AIR FRYER COOKBOOK FOR BEGINNERS

Poula Ray

© Copyright 2022 by Poula Ray - All rights reserved.

This document is geared towards providing exact and reliable information in regards to the topic and issue covered. The publication is sold with the idea that the publisher is not required to render accounting, officially permitted, or otherwise, qualified services. If advice is necessary, legal or professional, a practiced individual in the profession should be ordered.

- From a Declaration of Principles which was accepted and approved equally by a Committee of the American Bar Association and a Committee of Publishers and Associations.

In no way is it legal to reproduce, duplicate, or transmit any part of this document in either electronic means or in printed format. Recording of this publication is strictly prohibited and any storage of this document is not allowed unless with written permission from the publisher. All rights reserved.

The information provided herein is stated to be truthful and consistent, in that any liability, in terms of inattention or otherwise, by any usage or abuse of any policies, processes, or Instructions: contained within is the solitary and utter responsibility of the recipient reader. Under no circumstances will any legal responsibility or blame be held against the publisher for any reparation, damages, or monetary loss due to the information herein, either directly or indirectly.

Respective authors own all copyrights not held by the publisher.

The information herein is offered for informational purposes solely, and is universal as so. The presentation of the information is without contract or any type of guarantee assurance.

The trademarks that are used are without any consent, and the publication of the trademark is without permission or backing by the trademark owner. All trademarks and brands within this book are for clarifying purposes only and are the owned by the owners themselves, not affiliated with this document.

AIR FRYER COOKBOOK FOR BEGINNERS

TABLE OF CONTENTS

INTRODUCTION		6
BREAKFAST		7
1.	Yummy Bagel Morning	7
2.	Mustard Cheese Toast	7
3.	Potato Corn Frittata	8
4.	Tomato Cheese Sandwich	9
5.	Tofu Morning Treat	9
6.	Mushroom Eggs Morning	10
7.	Spinach Bacon Frittata	11
8.	Cream Sausage	11
9.	Quick Cheese Omelet	12
10.	Tomato Spinach Frittata	12
11.	Roasted Brussels Sprouts & Sweet Potatoes	13
12.	Roasted Potato Wedges	13
13.	Breakfast Egg Bites	14
14.	Grilled Cheese Sandwich	14
15.	Nuts and Seeds Granola	15
16.	Baked Eggs	15
17.	Eggs in Bread Cups	16
18.	Cream and Cheddar Omelet	17
19.	Bacon and Kale Frittata	17
20.	Sausage with Eggs	18
21.	Eggs With Chicken	18

22.	Air Fried Mushroom Frittata	19
23.	French Toast	20
24.	Breakfast Ham Omelet	20
25.	Crunchy Zucchini Hash Browns	21
26.	Crunchy Hash Browns	21
27.	Meaty Breakfast Omelet	22
28.	Citrus Blueberry Muffins	22
29.	Pb and J Donuts	23
30.	Breakfast Baked Apple	24

LUNCH — 26

31.	Pork Teriyaki	26
32.	Fajita Chicken Hasselback Chicken	27
33.	Pork Teriyaki Quesadillas	27
34.	Turkish Chicken Kebab Tavuk Shish	28
35.	Shrimp Southwestern Burritos	28
36.	Bacon Butter Burgers	29
37.	Mac and Cheese Eggrolls	30
38.	Mongolian Shrimp	30
39.	Chicken Asian Artichoke Burgers	31
40.	Blackened Lemon Salmon	32
41.	Crispy Beef and Bean Tacos	32
42.	Southwest Chicken Burritos	33
43.	Beef Bulgogi Burgers	34
44.	Broccoli and Cheese Stuffed Chicken	35
45.	Cajun Chicken Fried Steak Strips	35
46.	Meatballs Sandwich	36

47.	Bacon Pudding	37
48.	Coconut and Chicken Casserole	37
49.	Salmon and Asparagus	38
50.	Chicken and Corn Casserole	38
51.	Chicken and Zucchini Lunch Mix	39
52.	Chicken, Beans, Corn and Quinoa Casserole	40
53.	Roly-Poly Air Fried White Fish	40
54.	Air Fried Dragon Shrimp	41
55.	Coconut Lime Skirt Steak	42
56.	Honey Sea Bass	42
57.	Tuna Zucchini Melts	43
58.	Crispy Salt and Pepper Tofu	44
59.	Garlic Herb Butter Chicken Wings	44
60.	Beef Satay	45

DINNER 46

61.	Spicy Catfish	46
62.	BBQ Chicken Recipe from Greece	47
63.	Juicy Cheeseburgers	47
64.	Warming Winter Beef with Celery	48
65.	Air Fryer Vegetables	48
66.	Pork Meatballs	49
67.	Wondrous Creole Fried Shrimp with Sriracha Sauce	50
68.	Sesame Seeds Coated Fish	50
69.	Brine-Soaked Turkey	51
70.	Miso Glazed Salmon	52
71.	Lemon Chicken Breasts	52

72.	Breaded Cod	53
73.	Basil-Garlic Breaded Chicken Bake	54
74.	Cheeseburger Egg Rolls	54
75.	Creamy Burger and Potato Bake	55
76.	Roasted Heirloom Tomato with Baked Feta	56
77.	Stevia -Cajun Chicken Thighs	57
78.	Chicken Cordon Bleu	57
79.	Chicken Drumsticks	58
80.	Cajun Salmon	59
81.	Pistachio-Crusted Chicken Breast	59
82.	Garlic Lemon Pepper Scallops	60
83.	Chili Lime Chicken Thighs	60
84.	Spicy Lime Flank Steak	61
85.	Mustard-Glazed Pork Tenderloin	61
86.	Roasted Turkey Legs	62
DESSERT		63
87.	French Style Yogurt Treat	63
88.	Pineapple Cinnamon Treat	63
89.	Plum Apple Crumble	64
90.	Creamy Banana Puffs	65
91.	Choco-Berry Cake	66
92.	Pumpkin Pie Minis	66
93.	Mouthwatering Walnut Apple Pie Bites	67
94.	Gooey Apple Pie Cookies	67
95.	Apple Pie with Cinnamon Roll Crust	68
96.	Sugar Cookie Cake	69

97.	Apple Hand Pies	69
98.	Sweet Cream Cheese Wontons	69
99.	Cinnamon Sugar Roasted Chickpeas	70
100.	Brownie Muffins	70
101.	Chocolate Mug Cake	71
102.	Grilled Peaches	71
103.	Simple and Delicious Spiced Apples	72
104.	Tangy Mango Slices	72
105.	Peanut Butter Cookies	73
106.	Espresso Cinnamon Cookies	73
107.	Turmeric Almond Pie	74
108.	Sponge Cake	74
109.	Strawberry Cups	75
110.	Pecan Brownies	75
111.	Chocolate Banana Packets	76
112.	Creamy Strawberry Mini Wraps	76
113.	Heavenly Butter Cake Bars	77
114.	Tasty Shortbread Cookies	77
115.	Air-Fried Mini Pies	78
116.	Ricotta Stuffed Apples	78
117.	Banana-Almond Delights	78
CONCLUSION		80
INDEX		81

INTRODUCTION

An air fryer is a kitchen appliance designed to cook by circulating hot air around the food. Depending on the machine, this may be done in front of a mesh screen or in a rotating drum. This type of cooking allows for foods to be cooked with less oil than they would when deep fried, and without frying the food in oil at all. Air frying is also referred to as "air-circulating cooking" or "air-frying".

The air fryer has been around for about a decade, but it's only recently begun to appear on the grocery store shelves. This could be attributed to the fact that oil prices have risen and people are looking for more energy efficient ways of cooking. Most air fryers now cost less than $100 and operate on a fairly simple electric circuit with simple controls.

The air fryer works by circulating hot air around the food. Inside the interior of the machine is a basket and below that is a heating element. The basket has openings in it to allow the hot air to circulate through tightly packed foods like French fries, chicken nuggets, or vegetables. The food absorbs some of the oil used to coat it, then it's cooked right in front of your eyes.

If you are looking for a new way to cook foods without wasting oil and calories, then you will probably be interested in purchasing an air fryer. They have become popular for people that enjoy deep fried foods like fried chicken! But don't be fooled into thinking an air fryer only cooks fried foods. It can do a lot more than that. Air frying is ideal for many other things, like cooking French fries, chicken nuggets, and veggies! Why deep fry when you can cook food perfectly with just a simple appliance? Now you can prepare all kinds of foods in no time at all.

I decided to buy one for myself because it was a way to be healthy and delicious. To be honest, I don't really know much about the air fryer itself so I've done a lot of research to understand the best equipment and accessories for my purchase.

BREAKFAST

1. Yummy Bagel Morning

Preparation time: 8-10 minutes

Cooking time: 6 minutes

Servings: 5-6

Ingredients:
- 2 bagels, make halves
- 4 teaspoons butter

Directions:
1. Place your air fryer on a flat kitchen surface; plug it and turn it on. Set temperature to 370 degrees F and let it preheat for 4-5 minutes.
2. Take out the air-frying basket and gently coat it using a cooking oil or spray.
3. Add the bagels to the basket.
4. Push the air-frying basket in the air fryer. Let your air fryer cook the added bagels for 3 minutes.
5. Slide out the basket; spread the butter on over the bagels and cook for 3 more minutes.
6. Serve warm!

Nutrition: Calories: 258 Fat: 9 g Carbohydrates: 37 g Fiber: 2 g Protein: 7 g

2. Mustard Cheese Toast

Preparation time: 8-10 minutes

Cooking time: 15 minutes

Servings: 2

Ingredients:

- 2 eggs, whites, and yolks
- 1 tablespoon mustard
- 4 bread slices
- 2 tablespoons cheddar cheese, shredded
- 1 tablespoon paprika

Directions:

1. Place your air fryer on a flat kitchen surface; plug it and turn it on. Set temperature to 355 degrees F and let it preheat for 4-5 minutes.
2. Add the bread slice in the fryer basket. Cook for about 5 minutes or till toasted.
3. In a bowl of medium size, thoroughly whisk the egg whites.
4. In a bowl of medium size, thoroughly mix the cheese, egg yolks, mustard, and paprika.
5. Gently, fold in the egg whites.
6. Top the mustard mixture over the toasted bread. Cook for about 10 minutes.
7. Slide out the basket; serve warm!

Nutrition: Calories: 243 Fat: 7 g Carbohydrates: 31 g Fiber: 3 g Protein: 12 g

3. Potato Corn Frittata

Preparation time: 8-10 minutes

Cooking time: 10 minutes

Servings: 2

Ingredients:

- ½ cup frozen corn
- 1 large potato, boiled, peeled and cubed
- 3 jumbo eggs
- 1 tablespoon olive oil
- ½ of chorizo sausage, sliced
- 2 tablespoons feta cheese, crumbled
- 1 tablespoon fresh parsley, chopped
- Pepper and salt as needed

Directions:

1. Place your air fryer on a flat kitchen surface; plug it and turn it on. Set temperature to 355 degrees F and let it preheat for 4-5 minutes.
2. Take out the air-frying basket and add the oil.
3. Add the sausage, corn, and potato; cook for 5-6 minutes or till golden brown.
4. In a bowl of medium size, thoroughly whisk the eggs, salt, and pepper.
5. Add the egg mixture over the sausage mixture. Top with the cheese and parsley. Cook for about 5 minutes.
6. Slide out the basket; serve warm!

Nutrition: Calories: 445 Fat: 27 g Carbohydrates: 25 g Fiber: 2 g Protein: 20 g

4. Tomato Cheese Sandwich

Preparation time: 8-10 minutes

Cooking time: 6 minutes

Servings: 2

Ingredients:
- 8 tomato slices
- 4 bread slices
- 2 Swiss cheese slices
- Black pepper and salt as needed
- 4 teaspoons margarine

Directions:
1. Place your air fryer on a flat kitchen surface; plug it and turn it on. Set temperature to 355 degrees F and let it preheat for 4-5 minutes.
2. Take out the air-frying basket and gently coat it using a cooking oil or spray.
3. Add the1 cheese slice over 1 bread slice in the basket.
4. On top add 2 tomato slices and sprinkle with salt and pepper. Top with another bread slice.
5. Push the air-frying basket in the air fryer. Let your air fryer cook the added sandwich for the next 5 minutes.
6. Slide out the basket; spread 2 teaspoons of margarine on both sides of each sandwich. Cook for about 1 more minute.
7. Serve warm!

Nutrition: Calories: 369 Fat: 16 g Carbohydrates: 37 g Fiber: 5 g Protein: 14 g

5. Tofu Morning Treat

Preparation time: 5 minutes

Cooking time: 10 minutes

Servings: 2

Ingredients:
- ½ teaspoon sesame oil
- ½ teaspoon olive oil

- 8-ounce silken tofu, pressed and made slices
- 3 eggs
- 2 teaspoons fish sauce
- Black pepper as needed
- 1 teaspoon corn flour
- 2 teaspoons water

Directions:
1. Place your air fryer on a flat kitchen surface; plug it and turn it on. Set temperature to 390 degrees F and let it preheat for 4-5 minutes.
2. Take out the air-frying basket and gently coat it using a cooking oil or spray.
3. Add the tofu in the basket.
4. In a bowl of medium size, thoroughly whisk the corn flour into water.
5. In a bowl of large size, thoroughly mix the corn flour mixture, eggs, fish sauce, both oils, and pepper.
6. Add the eggs mixture over tofu.
7. Push the air-frying basket in the air fryer. Let your air fryer cook the added mixture for the next 10 minutes.
8. Slide out the basket; serve warm!

Nutrition: Calories: 244 Fat: 16 g Carbohydrates: 6 g Fiber: 0 g Protein: 22 g

6. Mushroom Eggs Morning

Preparation time: 5 minutes
Cooking time: 10 minutes
Servings: 2
Ingredients:
- ½ cup fresh mushrooms, chopped finely
- 4 eggs
- 2 tablespoons butter
- 2 tablespoons Parmesan cheese, shredded
- Pepper and salt as needed

Directions:

1. Place your air fryer on a flat kitchen surface; plug it and turn it on. Set temperature to 285 degrees F and let it preheat for 4-5 minutes.
2. Take out the air-frying basket and gently coat it using butter.
3. In a bowl of medium size, thoroughly whisk the eggs, salt, and black pepper.
4. Add the bow mixture in the basket.
5. Push the air-frying basket in the air fryer. Let your air fryer cook the added mixture for the next 5 minutes.
6. Slide out the basket; add the mushrooms and cook for 5 more minutes. Serve warm!

Nutrition: Calories: 271 Fat: 22 g Carbohydrates: 2 g Fiber: 0 g Protein: 16 g

7. Spinach Bacon Frittata

Preparation Time: 8-10 minutes

Cooking Time: 15 minutes

Servings: 2

Ingredients:
- ¼ cup green bell pepper, seeded and chopped
- 1 tablespoon olive oil
- ¼ cup spinach, chopped
- 2 bacon slices, chopped
- 4-6 cherry tomatoes, make halves
- 3 large eggs
- ¼ cup cheddar cheese, shredded

Directions:
1. Place your air fryer on a flat kitchen surface; plug it and turn it on. Set temperature to 360 degrees F and let it preheat for 4-5 minutes.
2. Take out the air-frying basket and gently coat it using a cooking oil or spray.
3. In a bowl of medium size, thoroughly mix the bacon, tomatoes and bell pepper.
4. Add the mixture to the basket.
5. Push the air-frying basket in the air fryer. Let your air fryer cook the added mixture for the next 8 minutes.
6. In a bowl of medium size, thoroughly mix the eggs, spinach, and cheese.
7. Slide out the basket; pour the egg mixture over the bacon mixture and cook for 8 more minutes.
8. Serve warm!

Nutrition: Calories: 482 Fat: 42 g Carbohydrates: 14 g Fiber: 5 g Protein: 28 g

8. Cream Sausage

Preparation time: 8-10 minutes

Cooking time: 20 minutes

Servings: 2-3

Ingredients:
- 2 cooked sausages, sliced
- 1 bread slice, make sticks
- ¼ cup cream
- 3 eggs
- ¼ cup mozzarella cheese, grated

Directions:
1. Place your air fryer on a flat kitchen surface; plug it and turn it on. Set temperature to 355 degrees F and let it preheat for 4-5 minutes.
2. Take 2 ramekins and gently grease them.
3. In a bowl of medium size, thoroughly whisk the cream and eggs. Add the egg mixture into ramekins.
4. Arrange the sausage slices and bread sticks around the edges; add them in the egg mixture.
5. Top with the cheese evenly. Add the ramekins in the basket.

6. Push the air-frying basket in the air fryer. Let your air fryer cook the added mixture for the next 20 minutes.
7. Slide out the basket; serve warm!

Nutrition: Calories: 476 Fat: 38 g Carbohydrates: 5 g Fiber: 0 g Protein: 24 g

9. Quick Cheese Omelet

Preparation time: 5 minutes

Cooking time: 9 minutes

Servings: 1

Ingredients:
- 2 eggs, lightly beaten
- ¼ cup cheddar cheese, shredded
- ¼ cup milk
- Pepper to taste
- Salt to taste

Direction:
1. In a bowl, whisk milk, eggs with pepper, and salt.
2. Spray small air fryer pan with cooking spray.
3. Pour egg mixture into the prepared pan and cook at 350 f for 6 minutes.
4. Sprinkle cheese on top and cook for 3 minutes more.
5. Serve and enjoy.

Nutrition: Calories 270, Fat 19.4 g, Carbohydrates 4.1 g, Sugar 3.6 g, Protein 20.1 g, Cholesterol 362 mg

10. Tomato Spinach Frittata

Preparation time: 10 minutes

Cooking time: 7 minutes

Servings: 1

Ingredients:
- 2 eggs, lightly beaten
- ¼ cup spinach, chopped

- ¼ cup tomatoes, chopped
- 2 tbsp. Milk
- 1 tbsp. Parmesan cheese, grated
- Pepper to taste
- Salt to taste

Direction:
1. In a medium bowl, whisk eggs. Add other ingredients and mix until well combined.
2. Spray small air fryer pan with cooking spray.
3. Pour egg mixture into the prepared pan and cook at 330 f for 7 minutes.
4. Serve and enjoy.

Nutrition: Calories189, Fat 11.7 g, Carbohydrates 4.3 g, Sugar 3.3 g, Protein15.7 g, Cholesterol 337 mg

11. Roasted Brussels Sprouts & Sweet Potatoes

Preparation time: 10 minutes
Cooking time: 20 minutes
Servings: 4
Ingredients:
- 1 lb. Brussels sprouts, cut in half
- 2 sweet potatoes, wash and cut into 1-inch pieces
- 2 tbsp. Olive oil
- ¼ tsp garlic powder
- ½ tsp pepper
- 1 tsp salt

Direction:
1. Add sweet potatoes and brussels sprouts in the mixing bowl.
2. Add remaining ingredients over sweet potatoes and brussels sprouts and toss until well coated.
3. Transfer sweet potatoes and brussels sprouts on air fryer oven tray and roast at 400 f for 10 minutes.
4. Turn sweet potatoes and brussels sprouts to the other side and roast for 10 minutes more.
5. Serve and enjoy.

Nutrition: Calories138, Fat 7.4 g, Carbohydrates 17.2 g, Sugar 3.9 g, Protein4.4 g, Cholesterol 0 mg

12. Roasted Potato Wedges

Preparation time: 10 minutes

Cooking time: 10 minutes

Servings: 6

Ingredients:

- 2 lbs. Potatoes, cut into wedges
- 2 tbsp. McCormick's chipotle seasoning
- ¼ cup olive oil

Direction:

1. Add potato wedges into the mixing bowl.
2. Add remaining ingredients over potato wedges and toss until well coated.
3. Transfer potato wedges onto the air fryer oven tray roast at 400 f for 5 minutes.
4. Turn potato wedges to the other side and roast for 5 minutes more.
5. Serve and enjoy.

Nutrition: Calories176, Fat 8.6 g, Carbohydrates 23.8 g, Sugar 1.7 g, Protein2.5 g, Cholesterol 0 mg

13. Breakfast Egg Bites

Preparation time: 10 minutes

Cooking time: 13 minutes

Servings: 4

Ingredients:

- 4 eggs, lightly beaten
- ¼ cup ham, diced
- ¼ cup cheddar cheese, shredded
- ¼ cup bell pepper, diced
- ½ cup milk
- Pepper to taste
- Salt to taste

Direction:

1. Add all necessary ingredients into the mixing bowl and whisk until well combined.

2. Spray muffin silicone mold with cooking spray.
3. Pour egg mixture into the silicone muffin mold and place it in the air fryer oven and bake at 350 f for 10 minutes.
4. After 10 minutes flip egg bites and cook for 3 minutes more. Serve and enjoy.

Nutrition: Calories123, Fat 8.1 g, Carbohydrates 2.8 g, Sugar 2.1 g, Protein9.8 g, Cholesterol 178 mg

14. Grilled Cheese Sandwich

Preparation time: 5 minutes
Cooking time: 4 minutes
Servings: 2
Ingredients:
- 4 Texas toast slices
- 4 Colby jack cheese slices

Direction:
1. Spray air fryer oven tray with cooking spray.
2. Place two toast slices on a tray then top with cheese slices.
3. Now place remaining toast slices on top of the cheese.
4. Air fry at 400 f for 4 minutes.
5. Serve and enjoy.

Nutrition: Calories225, Fat 4 g, Carbohydrates 38.5 g, Sugar 4 g, Protein8.5 g, Cholesterol 5 mg

15. Nuts and Seeds Granola

Preparation time: 10 minutes
Cooking time: 15 minutes
Servings: 8
Ingredients:
- 1/3 cup canola oil
- ¼ cup maple syrup
- 2 tablespoons honey
- ½ teaspoon vanilla extract

- 2 cups rolled oats
- ½ cup wheat germ, toasted
- ¼ cup dried cherries
- ¼ cup dried blueberries
- 2 tablespoons dried cranberries
- 2 tablespoons sunflower seeds
- 2 tablespoons pumpkin seeds, shelled
- 1 tablespoon flaxseed
- 2 tablespoons pecans, chopped
- 2 tablespoons hazelnuts, chopped
- 2 tablespoons almonds, chopped
- 2 tablespoons walnuts, chopped
- ½ teaspoon ground cinnamon

Direction:
1. In a small bowl, add the oil and maple syrup and mix well.
2. In a large bowl, add the remaining ingredients and mix well.
3. Add the oil mixture and mix until well combined.
4. Place the mixture into a baking dish that will fit in the iconites air fryer oven.
5. Select "air fry" of iconites air fryer toaster oven and then adjust the temperature to 350 degrees f.
6. Set the timer for 15 minutes and press "start" to preheat.
7. After preheating, insert the baking dish in the center position of oven.
8. Stir the granola after every 5 minutes.
9. When cooking time is complete, remove the baking dish from oven.
10. set the granola side to cool completely before
11. Serving.

Nutrition: Calories302, Total Fat 16.1 g, Saturated Fat 2.1 g, Cholesterol 0 mg, Sodium 4 mg, Total Carbs 35.1 g, Fiber 5.7 g, Sugar 14 g, Protein6.9 g

16. Baked Eggs

Preparation time: 10 minutes
Cooking time: 12 minutes

Servings: 4

Ingredients:
- 1 cup marinara sauce, divided
- 1 tablespoon capers, drained and divided
- 8 eggs
- ¼ cup whipping cream, divided
- ¼ cup parmesan cheese, shredded and divided
- Salt and ground black pepper, as required

Direction:
1. Grease 4 ramekins. Set aside.
2. Divide the marinara sauce in the bottom of each prepared ramekin evenly and top with capers.
3. Carefully, crack 2 eggs over marinara sauce into each ramekin and top with cream, followed by the parmesan cheese.
4. Sprinkle each ramekin with salt and black pepper.
5. Select "bake" of iconites air fryer oven and then adjust the temperature to 400 degrees f.
6. Set the timer for 12 minutes and press "start" to preheat.
7. After preheating, arrange the ramekins over the wire rack and insert in the oven.
8. When cooking time is complete, remove the ramekins from oven.
9. Serve warm.

Nutrition: Calories 223, Total Fat 14.1 g, Saturated Fat 5.5 g, Cholesterol 341 mg, Sodium 569 mg, Total Carbs 9.8 g, Fiber 1.7 g, Sugar 6.2 g, Protein 14.3 g

17. Eggs in Bread Cups

Preparation time: 10 minutes

Cooking time: 23 minutes

Servings: 4

Ingredients:
- 4 bacon slices
- 2 bread slices, crust removed
- 4 eggs
- Salt and ground black pepper, as required

Direction:
1. Grease 4 cups of muffin tin and set aside.
2. Heat a small frying pan over medium-high heat and cook the bacon slices for about 2-3 minutes.
3. With a slotted spoon, transfer the bacon slice onto a paper towel-lined plate to cool.
4. Break each bread slice in half.
5. Arrange 1 bread slices half in each of prepared muffin cup and press slightly.
6. Now, arrange 1 bacon slice over each bread slice in a circular shape.
7. Crack 1 egg into each muffin cup and sprinkle with salt and black pepper.
8. Select "bake" of iconites air fryer oven and then adjust the temperature to 350 degrees f.
9. Set the timer for 20 minutes and press "start" to preheat.
10. After preheating, arrange the muffin tin over the wire rack and insert in the oven.
11. When cooking time is complete, remove the muffin tin from oven.
12. Serve warm.

Nutrition: Calories 98, Total Fat 6.6 g, Saturated Fat 2.1 g, Cholesterol 168 mg, Sodium 206 mg, Total Carbs 2.6 g, Fiber 0.1 g, Sugar 0.5 g, Protein7.3 g

18. Cream and Cheddar Omelet

Preparation time: 10 minutes
Cooking time: 8 minutes
Servings: 2
Ingredients:
- 4 eggs
- ¼ cup cream
- Salt and ground black pepper, as required
- ¼ cup cheddar cheese, grated

Direction:
1. In a bowl, add the eggs, cream, salt, and black pepper and beat until well combined.
2. Place the egg mixture into a small baking pan.
3. Select "air fry" of iconites air fryer oven and then adjust the temperature to 350 degrees f.
4. Set the timer for 8 minutes and press "start" to preheat.
5. After preheating, arrange the baking pan over the wire rack and insert in the oven.

6. After 4 minutes, sprinkle the omelet with cheese evenly.
7. When cooking time is complete, remove the baking pan from oven.
8. Cut the omelet into 2 portions and serve hot.

Nutrition: Calories 88, Total Fat 15.1 g, Saturated Fat 6.8 g, Cholesterol 348 mg, Sodium 298 mg, Total Carbs 1.8 g, Fiber 0 g, Sugar 1.4 g, Protein14.8 g

19. Bacon and Kale Frittata

Preparation time: 10 minutes

Cooking time: 16 minutes

Servings: 2

Ingredients:
- ¼ cup bacon, chopped
- ¼ cup fresh kale, tough ribs removed and chopped
- ½ of tomato, cubed
- 3 eggs
- Salt and ground black pepper, as required
- ¼ cup parmesan cheese, grated

Direction:
1. Heat a nonstick skillet over medium heat and cook the bacon for about 5 minutes.
2. Add the kale and cook for about 1-2 minutes.
3. Add the tomato and cook for about 2-3 minutes.
4. Remove from the heat and drain the grease from skillet.
5. Set aside to cool slightly.
6. Meanwhile, in a small bowl, add the eggs, salt and black pepper and beat well.
7. In a greased baking dish, place the bacon mixture and top with the eggs, followed by the cheese.
8. Select "air fry" of iconites air fryer oven and then adjust the temperature to 355 degrees f.
9. Set the timer for 8 minutes and press "start" to preheat.
10. after preheating, arrange the baking dish in the center of oven.
11. when cooking time is complete, remove the baking dish from oven.
12. cut into equal-sized wedges and serve.

Nutrition: Calories 293, Total Fat 19.7 g, Saturated Fat 9.8 g, Cholesterol 279 mg, Sodium 935 mg, Total Carbs 3.4 g, Fiber 0.3 g, Sugar 0.9 g, Protein25.4 g

20. Sausage with Eggs

Preparation time: 10 minutes

Cooking time: 6 minutes

Servings: 2

Ingredients:

- 4 breakfast sausage
- 2 hard-boiled eggs, peeled
- 1 avocado, peeled, pitted and sliced

Direction:

1. Arrange the sausages in the rotisserie basket and attach the lid.
2. Arrange the drip pan in the bottom of instant iconites air fryer oven cooking chamber.
3. Select "roast" of iconites air fryer oven and then adjust the temperature to 375 degrees f.
4. Set the timer for 6 minutes and press "start" to preheat.
5. After preheating, arrange the rotisserie basket, on the rotisserie spit.
6. Then, close the door and touch "rotate".
7. When cooking time is complete, press the red lever to release the rod.
8. Remove from the oven and place the sausages onto
9. Serving plates.
10. Divide eggs and avocado slices onto each plate and serve.

Nutrition: Calories 322, Total Fat 28.5 g, Saturated Fat 6.9 g, Cholesterol 177 mg, Sodium 187 mg, Total Carbs 9 g, Fiber 6.7 g, Sugar 0.8 g, Protein10.6 g

21. Eggs With Chicken

Preparation time: 10 minutes

Cooking time: 12 minutes

Servings: 3

Ingredients:
- 4 large eggs, divided
- 2 tablespoons heavy cream
- Salt and ground black pepper, as required
- 2 teaspoons unsalted butter, softened
- 2 ounces cooked chicken, chopped
- 3 tablespoons parmesan cheese, grated finely
- 2 teaspoons fresh parsley, minced

Direction:
1. In a bowl, add 1 egg, cream, salt and black pepper and beat until smooth.
2. In the bottom of a pie pan, place the butter and spread evenly.
3. In the bottom of pie pan, place chicken over butter and top with the egg mixture evenly.
4. Carefully, crack the remaining eggs on top.
5. Sprinkle with salt and black pepper and top with cheese and parsley evenly.
6. Select "air fry" of iconites air fryer oven and then adjust the temperature to 320 degrees f.
7. Set the timer for 12 minutes and press "start" to preheat.
8. After preheating, arrange pan over the wire rack and insert in the oven.
9. When cooking time is complete, remove the pan from oven.
10. cut into equal-sized wedges and serve hot.

Nutrition: Calories 199, Total Fat 14.7 g, Saturated Fat 6.7 g, Cholesterol 287 mg, Sodium 221 mg, Total Carbs 0.8 g, Fiber 0 g, Sugar 0.5 g, Protein 16.1 g

22. Air Fried Mushroom Frittata

Preparation time: 10 minutes

Cooking time: 12 minutes

Servings: 2

Ingredients:
- 4 egg whites
- 1/3 cup mushrooms, sliced
- 1 large tomato, sliced
- ¼ cup finely chopped chives
- 2 tbsp. Milk
- Salt and freshly ground black pepper to taste

Direction:
1. Start by setting your air fryer toast oven to 320 f.
2. Beat the egg whites and milk in a large bowl. Add in the fresh ingredients and mix until well combined then set the bowl aside.
3. Lightly grease your air fryer toast oven's frying pan and transfer the egg mixture into the pan.
4. Cook in the fryer for about 10 -12 minutes or until done to desire.

Nutrition: Calories: 360 K Cal, Carbs: 10.8 g, Fat: 28.6 g, Protein: 4.6 g

23. French Toast

Preparation time: 10 minutes
Cooking time: 20 minutes
Servings: 3

Ingredients:
- 6 slices of preferred bread
- ¾ cup of milk
- 3 eggs
- 1 tsp. Pure vanilla extract
- 1 tbsp. Ground cinnamon

Direction:
1. Start by preheating your air fryer toast oven at 320 degrees f.
2. Combine all the ingredients apart from the bread in a medium bowl until well mixed.
3. Dunk each slice of bread into the egg mix, gently shake the excess off and place in a greased pan.
4. Cook in the fryer, each side for 3 minutes and repeat for the remaining slices.
5. To serve, drizzle with maple syrup.

Nutrition: Calories: 245 K Cal, Carbs: 28.5 g, Fat: 7.5 g, Protein: 14.9 g.

24. Breakfast Ham Omelet

Preparation time: 10 minutes

Cooking time: 10 minutes

Servings: 2

Ingredients:
- 3 large eggs
- 100g ham, cut into small pieces
- ¼ cup milk
- ¾ cup mixed vegetables (white mushrooms, green onions, red pepper)
- ¼ cup mixed cheddar and mozzarella cheese
- 1 tsp. Freshly chopped mixed herbs (cilantro and chives)
- Salt and freshly ground pepper to taste

Direction:
1. Combine the eggs and milk in a medium bowl then add in the remaining ingredients apart from the cheese and mixed herbs and beat well using a fork.
2. Pour the egg mix into an evenly greased pan then place it in the basket of your air fryer toast oven.
3. Cook for roughly 10 minutes at 350 degrees f or until done to desire.
4. Sprinkle the cheese and mixed herbs on the omelet halfway through cooking time.
5. Gently loosen the omelet from the sides of the pan using a spatula.
6. Serve hot!

Nutrition: Calories: 411 K Cal, Carbs: 14 g, Fat: 39.3 g, Protein: 28 g

25. Crunchy Zucchini Hash Browns

Preparation time: 10 minutes

Cooking time: 15 minutes

Servings: 3

Ingredients:
- 4 medium zucchinis, peeled and grated

- 1 tsp. Onion powder
- 1 tsp. Garlic powder
- 2 tbsp. Almond flour
- 1 ½ tsp. Chili flakes
- Salt and freshly ground pepper to taste
- 2 tsp. Olive oil

Direction:
1. Put the grated zucchini in between layers of kitchen towel and squeeze to drain excess water.
2. Pour 1 teaspoon of oil in a pan, preferably non-stick, over medium heat and sauté the potatoes for about 3 minutes.
3. Transfer the zucchini to a shallow bowl and let cool. Sprinkle the zucchini with the remaining ingredients and mix until well combined.
4. Transfer the zucchini mix to a flat plate and pat it down to make 1 compact layer. Put in the fridge and let it sit for 20 minutes.
5. Set your air fryer toast oven to 360 degrees f.
6. Meanwhile take out the flattened zucchini and divide into equal portions using a knife or cookie cutter.
7. Lightly brush your air fryer toast oven's basket with the remaining teaspoon of olive oil.
8. Gently place the zucchini pieces into the greased basket and fry for 12-15 minutes, flipping the hash browns halfway through.
9. Enjoy hot!

Nutrition: Calories: 195 K Cal, Carbs: 10.4 g, Fat: 13.1 g, Protein: 9.6 g

26. Crunchy Hash Browns

Preparation time: 10 minutes
Cooking time: 15 minutes
Servings: 3
Ingredients:
- 5 medium potatoes, peeled and grated
- 1 tsp. Onion powder
- 1 tsp. Garlic powder

- 2 tbsp. Corn flour
- 1 ½ tsp. Chili flakes
- Salt and freshly ground pepper to taste
- 2 tsp. Olive oil

Direction:

1. Put the grated potatoes in a large bowl and cover with ice cold water and let it sit for a minute. Drain the water and repeat this step two times. (This helps in eliminating the excess starch)
2. Pour 1 teaspoon of oil in a pan, preferably non-stick, over medium heat and sauté the potatoes for about 3 minutes.
3. Transfer the potatoes to a shallow bowl and let cool. Sprinkle the potatoes with the remaining ingredients and mix until well combined.
4. Transfer the potato mix to a flat plate and pat it down to make 1 compact layer. Put in the fridge and let it sit for 20 minutes.
5. Set your air fryer toast oven to 360 degrees f.
6. Meanwhile take out the flattened potato and divide into equal portions using a knife or cookie cutter.
7. Lightly brush your air fryer toast oven's basket with the remaining teaspoon of olive oil.
8. Gently place the potato pieces into the greased basket and fry for 12-15 minutes, flipping the hash browns halfway through.
9. Enjoy hot!

Nutrition: Calories: 295 K Cal, Carbs: 60.9 g, Fat: 3.7 g, Protein: 6.6 g.

27. Meaty Breakfast Omelet

Preparation time: 10 minutes

Cooking time: 10 minutes

Servings: 2

Ingredients:

- 3 large eggs
- 100g ham, cut into small pieces
- ¼ cup milk
- ¾ cup mixed vegetables (mushrooms, scallions, bell pepper)
- ¼ cup mixed cheddar and mozzarella cheese

- 1 tsp. Mixed herbs
- Salt and freshly ground pepper to taste

Direction:

1. Combine the eggs and milk in a medium bowl then add in the remaining ingredients apart from the cheese and mixed herbs and beat well using a fork.
2. Pour the egg mix into an evenly greased pan then place it in the basket of your air fryer toast oven.
3. Cook for roughly 10 minutes at 350 degrees f or until done to desire.
4. Sprinkle the cheese and mixed herbs on the omelet halfway through cooking time:
5. Gently loosen the omelet from the sides of the pan using a spatula.
6. Serve hot!

Nutrition: Calories: 278 K Cal, Carbs: 1.3 g, Fat: 4.6 g, Protein: 24.1 g.

28. Citrus Blueberry Muffins

Preparation time: 10 minutes

Cooking time: 15 minutes

Servings: 3-4

Ingredients:

- 2 ½ cups cake flour
- ½ cup Sugar
- ¼ cup light cooking oil such as avocado oil
- ½ cup heavy cream
- 1 cup fresh blueberries
- 2 eggs
- Zest and juice from 1 orange
- 1 tsp. Pure vanilla extract
- 1 tsp. Brown Sugar for topping

Direction:

1. Start by combining the oil, heavy cream, eggs, orange juice and vanilla extract in a large bowl then set aside.
2. Separately combine the flour and Sugar until evenly mixed then pour little by little into the wet ingredients.

3. Combine well unlit well blended but careful not to over mix.
4. Preheat your air fryer toast oven at 320 degrees f
5. Gently fold the blueberries into the batter and divide into cupcake holders, preferably, silicone cupcake holders as you won't have to grease them. Alternatively, you can use cupcake paper liners on any cupcake holders
6. Tray you could be having.
7. Sprinkle the tops with the brown Sugar and pop the muffins in the fryer.
8. Bake for about 12 minutes. Use a toothpick to check for readiness. When the muffins have evenly browned and an inserted toothpick comes out clean, they are ready.
9. Take out the muffins and let cool.
10. Enjoy!

Nutrition: Calories: 289 K Cal, Carbs: 12.8 g, Fat: 32 g, Protein: 21.1 g.

29. Pb and J Donuts

Preparation time: 10 minutes

Cooking time: 12 minutes

Servings: 4

Ingredients:

For the donuts:
- 1 ¼ cups all-purpose flour
- ½ tsp. baking soda
- ½ tsp. baking powder
- 1/3 cup Sugar
- ½ cup buttermilk
- 1 large egg
- 1 tsp. Pure vanilla extract
- 3 tbsp. Unsalted, melted and divided into 2+1
- ¾ tsp. Salt

For the glaze:
- 2 tbsp. Milk
- ½ cup powdered Sugar

- 2 tbsp. Smooth peanut butter
- Sea salt to taste

For the filling:
- ½ cup strawberry or blueberry jelly

Direction:
1. Whisk together all the dry ingredients for the donut in a large bowl.
2. Separately combine the egg, buttermilk, melted butter and vanilla extract.
3. Create a small well at the center of the dry ingredients and pour in the egg mixture. Use a fork to combine the ingredients then finish off with a spatula.
4. Place the dough on a floured surface and knead the dough. It will start out sticky but as you knead, it's going to come together.
5. Roll out the dough to make a ¾ inch thick circle. Use a cookie cutter, or the top part of a cup to cut the dough into rounds.
6. Place the donuts on a parchment paper and then into your air fryer toast oven. You may have to cook in batches depending on the size of your air fryer toast oven.
7. Cook for 12 minutes at 350 degrees f.
8. Use a pastry bag or squeeze bottle to fill the donuts with jelly.
9. Combine the glaze ingredients and drizzle on top of the donuts. enjoy!

Nutrition: Calories: 430 K Cal, Carbs: 66.8 g, Fat: 14.6 g, Protein: 9.1 g.

30. Breakfast Baked Apple

Preparation time: 10 minutes
Cooking time: 20 minutes
Servings: 2
Ingredients:
- 1 apple
- 2 tbsp. Raisins
- 2 tbsp. Walnuts, chopped
- ¼ tsp. Nutmeg
- ¼ tsp. Ground cinnamon
- 1 ½ tsp. Margarine

- ¼ Cup water

Direction:

1. Start by setting your air fryer toast oven to 350 degrees f.
2. Cut the apple in half and gently spoon out some of the flesh.
3. Place the apple halves on your air fryer toast ovens frying pan.
4. Mix the raisins, walnuts, nutmeg, cinnamon and margarine in a bowl and divide equally between the apple halves.
5. Pour the water into the pan and cook for 20 minutes.
6. Enjoy!

Nutrition: Calories: 161 K Cal, Carbs: 23.7 g, Fat: 7.8 g, Protein: 2.5g

LUNCH

31. Pork Teriyaki

Preparation time: 15 minutes
Cooking time: 30 minutes
Servings: 4
Ingredients:
- 2 tablespoons soy sauce
- 2 tablespoons coconut aminos
- 1 tablespoon olive oil
- 1 tablespoon honey
- 1 tablespoon bourbon
- 1 tablespoon rice vinegar
- 2 cloves garlic, minced
- 1 tablespoon ginger, grated
- 1 teaspoon salt
- 1/2 teaspoon black pepper
- 1 lb. pork tenderloin

Directions:

1. Whisk the soy sauce, coconut aminos, olive oil, honey, bourbon, rice vinegar, garlic, ginger, salt, and pepper in a large bowl.
2. Add the pork tenderloin, cover with plastic wrap, and chill it in the fridge overnight.
3. Set your oven to 400F/205C for 5 minutes. Add the pork teriyaki to the air fryer's basket and cook for 20-25 minutes. Let the pork tenderloin rest 5-10 minutes before carving.

Nutrition: Calories: 105 Carbs: 2 g Fat: 3 g Protein: 18 g

32. Fajita Chicken Hasselback Chicken

Preparation time: 15 minutes
Cooking time: 12-15 minutes
Servings: 2
Ingredients:
- 1 teaspoon salt
- 1/2 teaspoon black pepper
- 1 teaspoon garlic powder
- 1 teaspoon onion powder
- 1 teaspoon smoked paprika
- 1 teaspoon fajita seasoning
- 4 ounces provolone cheese, sliced into pieces
- 1/2 small green bell pepper, thinly sliced
- 1/4 small red onion, thinly sliced
- 2 boneless, skinless chicken breasts

Directions:
1. Whisk the salt, pepper, garlic powder, onion powder, smoked paprika, fajita seasoning in a small bowl.
2. Slice six slits crosswise on each chicken breast without cutting all the way through. Season the chicken breast with the fajita seasoning mix.
3. Stuff each slit on the chicken with 1 strip of red onion, 1 piece of provolone cheese, and 1 strip of green pepper.
4. Place the fajita chicken Hasselback chicken into the air fryer's basket. Cook the fajita chicken Hasselback chicken for 12-15 minutes at 350F/177C.

Nutrition: Calories: 269 Carbs: 3 g Fat: 9 g Protein: 34 g

33. Pork Teriyaki Quesadillas

Preparation time: 10 minutes
Cooking time: 5 minutes
Servings: 2-3
Ingredients:
- 1 tablespoon butter, softened
- 1 large flour tortilla
- 1/2 cup cheddar cheese, shredded
- 1/4 cup Mexican cheese
- 2 tablespoons green salsa
- 1/2 cup pork teriyaki, shredded

Directions:
1. Spread the softened butter onto one-half of the tortilla. Place the cheese onto one half of the tortilla and top with the salsa and pork teriyaki.
2. Fold the filling-free side of the tortilla over the pork teriyaki and place the tortilla into the air fryer basket.
3. Cook the quesadilla for 2 minutes at 350F/177C, remove it from the air fryer and press down if the top half of the quesadilla has lifted. Cook the quesadilla for another 2-3 minutes. Serve.

Nutrition: Calories: 240 Carbs: 29 g Fat: 9 g Protein: 12 g

34. Turkish Chicken Kebab Tavuk Shish

Preparation time: 10 minutes
Cooking time: 15 minutes
Servings: 4
Ingredients:
- 1/4 cup plain Greek yogurt
- 2 cloves garlic, minced
- 1 tablespoon tomato paste
- 1 tablespoon olive oil
- 1 tablespoon lime zest

- 1 tablespoon lime juice
- 1 teaspoon sea salt
- 1 teaspoon coriander
- 1 teaspoon smoked paprika
- 1/2 teaspoon nutmeg
- 1/2 teaspoon black pepper
- 1 lb. boneless skinless chicken thighs, cut into 1-1 1/2- inch pieces

Directions:
1. Whisk the Greek yogurt, garlic, tomato paste, lime juice, lime zest, olive oil, salt, coriander, paprika, nutmeg, and black pepper in a large bowl, then add the chicken thighs.
2. Mix the chicken thighs to coat them in the marinade and let them rest for 30 minutes or overnight in the refrigerator.
3. Place the marinated chicken thighs into the air fryer's basket in an even layer and cook for 10 minutes at 370F/188C.
4. Turn the Turkish chicken thighs over and cook for additional 5-6 minutes until it has a temperature of 165F.

Nutrition: Calories: 381 Carbs: 1 g Fat: 12 g Protein: 67 g

35. Shrimp Southwestern Burritos

Preparation time: 10 minutes

Cooking time: 20 minutes

Servings: 6

Ingredients:
- 1 lb. jumbo shrimp, cooked, chopped into bite-sized pieces
- 8 oz. cream cheese, softened
- 1½ cups shredded Mozzarella cheese, shredded
- 1 cup black beans, drained and rinsed
- 1 15 oz. can sweet corn, drained
- 1 14 oz. can fire-roasted diced tomatoes, drained
- 2 tablespoons old bay seasoning
- 1 tablespoon lemon juice

- 1 cup fresh Pico de Gallo
- 6 flour tortillas, burrito size

Directions:
1. Set the air fryer to 400F/205C. Mix the shrimp, cream cheese, mozzarella cheese, black beans, sweet corn, tomatoes, old bay seasoning, and Pico de Gallo in a bowl.
2. Place 1 cup of the shrimp filling in the middle of each tortilla, then fold the edges of the tortilla over, and roll it up.
3. Mist the shrimp burrito with olive oil spray, then place it into the air fryer's basket. Cook the shrimp burritos for 5 minutes, turn them over and cook for additional 5 minutes.

Nutrition: Calories: 303 Carbs: 62 g Fat: 4 g Protein: 14 g

36. Bacon Butter Burgers

Preparation time: 10 minutes
Cooking time: 14 minutes
Servings: 2
Ingredients:
- 1 lb. lean ground beef
- 1/2 cup frozen butter cut into small cubes
- 1 teaspoon sea salt
- 1/2 teaspoon black pepper
- 1 teaspoon garlic powder
- 1 teaspoon onion powder
- 1 teaspoon smoked paprika
- 2 hamburger buns
- 2 slices thick-cut bacon, cooked

Directions:
1. Combine the beef, butter, salt, pepper, garlic powder, onion powder, and smoked paprika in a bowl.
2. Shape the burger mixture into two patties about 1-inch in thickness. Spray the air fryer's basket with olive oil, then mist the patties with olive oil spray.
3. Cook the butter burgers for 7 minutes at 375F/191C, then turn them over and cook for additional 7 minutes.

4. Place the butter burgers onto the buns, top with bacon, and your favorite burger toppings.

Nutrition: Calories: 105 Carbs: 3 g Fat: 8 g Protein: 5 g

37. Mac and Cheese Eggrolls

Preparation time: 10 minutes

Cooking time: 8 minutes

Servings: 8

Difficulty: Easy

Ingredients:

- 3 cups cooked macaroni and cheese
- 1/2 cup shredded cheddar cheese
- 1/2 cup Fontina cheese, shredded
- ½ cup shredded mozzarella cheese
- 1 teaspoon salt
- 1/2 teaspoon black pepper
- 1 tablespoon hot sauce
- 16 egg roll wrappers
- 2 tablespoons water

Directions:

1. Combine the macaroni & cheese, cheddar cheese, fontina cheese, mozzarella cheese, salt, black pepper, and hot sauce. Arrange the eggroll wrappers onto a flat surface.
2. Add two tablespoons of mac and cheese filling to the center of each eggroll wrapper.

3. Fold the ends of the eggroll wrapper over the filling and roll it up, dabbing the free edge with a bit of water to seal it.
4. Mist the air fryer's basket with oil, then add the mac and cheese egg rolls to the basket. Mist the egg rolls with olive oil spray and cook them for 4 minutes at 390F/199C.
5. Turn the mac and cheese egg rolls over and cook for additional 4 minutes.

Nutrition: Calories: 80 Carbs: 11 g Fat: 5 g Protein: 3 g

38. Mongolian Shrimp

Preparation time: 10 minutes
Cooking time: 15 minutes
Servings: 4
Ingredients:
- 1 lb. jumbo shrimp, peeled, deveined
- 4 tablespoons cornstarch
- 2 tablespoons olive oil
- 4 cloves garlic, minced
- 2 tablespoons ginger, minced
- 1/4 cup soy sauce
- 1/4 cup coconut aminos
- 1/2 cup water
- 1/2 cup maple syrup

Directions:
1. Toss the shrimp in the cornstarch, then let it sit for 5 minutes. Set the air fryer to 400F/205C. Add the shrimp to the air fryer's basket and mist it liberally with olive oil spray.
2. Cook the shrimp for 6-8 minutes, shaking the basket every 3 minutes. Place the oil in a skillet over medium-high heat, add ginger and garlic, and cook for 30 seconds to 1 minute.
3. Stir in the soy sauce, coconut aminos, water, and maple syrup, and simmer it for 6-7 minutes, stirring every so often until it thickens.
4. Add the shrimp to the Mongolian sauce, toss to coat and cook for 1-2 minutes.

Nutrition: Calories: 230 Carbs: 19 g Fat: 10 g Protein: 15 g

39. Chicken Asian Artichoke Burgers

Preparation time: 10 minutes

Cooking time: 0 minutes

Servings: 2

Ingredients:

- 1/2 lb. raw ground chicken
- 1/4 cup artichokes, chopped
- 1/4 cup shallots minced
- 2 tablespoons sweet chili sauce
- 2 tablespoons soy sauce
- 2 hamburger buns

Directions:

1. Mix the ground chicken, artichokes, shallots, sweet chili sauce, and soy sauce in a bowl. Form the ground chicken mixture into 2 patties that are about 1/2-inch in thickness.
2. Spray your air fryer's basket with nonstick spray. Add the Asian chicken patties to the basket and cook them for 12 minutes at 392F/200C.
3. Place the Chicken Asian Artichoke Burgers onto the buns and top with your favorite burger toppings.

Nutrition: Calories: 230 Carbs: 23 g Fat: 13 g Protein: 6 g

40. Blackened Lemon Salmon

Preparation time: 10 minutes

Cooking time: 8 minutes

Servings: 2-3

Ingredients:

- 2 8oz. salmon filets
- 1 teaspoon salt
- 1 teaspoon chili powder
- 1 teaspoon onion powder
- 1 teaspoon paprika
- 1 teaspoon lemon pepper

- zest of 1 lemon
- juice of 1 lemon

Directions:

1. Whisk the salt, chili powder, onion powder, paprika, lemon pepper, and lemon zest in a small bowl. Set the air fryer 390F/199C.
2. Pat the salmon fillets fry using paper towels and generously rub the blackening season all over the salmon fillets.
3. Mist the air fryer's basket with olive oil and add the salmon fillets to the basket skin side down. Mist the salmon fillets with olive oil.
4. Cook the blackened salmon for 8 minutes until the salmon has a temperature is 145F. Transfer the blackened lemon salmon to a plate and squeeze the lemon juice on top.

Nutrition: Calories: 233 Carbs: 1 g Fat: 12 g Protein: 28 g

41. Crispy Beef and Bean Tacos

Preparation time: 15 minutes

Cooking time: 20 minutes

Servings: 10

Ingredients:

- 10 stand and stuff taco shells
- 1 tablespoon olive oil
- 1 lb. lean ground beef
- 12 cloves garlic minced
- 1/2 small onion, minced
- 1 tablespoon chili powder
- 1 teaspoon smoked paprika
- 1/2 teaspoon coriander
- 1 teaspoon onion powder
- 1 teaspoon garlic powder
- 1 cup black beans, drained, rinsed
- 1 cup shredded sharp cheddar cheese

Directions:

1. Place the ground beef and olive oil in a skillet and brown it over medium-high heat for 5-10 minutes, breaking it into smaller chunks.
2. Drain the ground beef, then stir in the onion, garlic, chili powder, smoked paprika, coriander, onion powder, garlic powder, and black beans. Cook for 5-6 minutes until the onions soften.
3. Set the air fryer to 375F. Stuff the taco shells with ground beef black bean mixture, then top with the cheddar cheese.
4. Place the crispy beef and bean tacos into the air fryer's basket and cook for 3-4 minutes until the cheese melts.

Nutrition: Calories: 340 Carbs: 35 g Fat: 13 g Protein: 22 g

42. Southwest Chicken Burritos

Preparation time: 10 minutes
Cooking time: 10 minutes
Servings: 6
Ingredients:
- 2 cups cooked shredded chicken
- 8 oz. cream cheese, softened
- 1½ cups shredded Mexican cheese, shredded
- 1 cup black beans, drained and rinsed
- 1 15 oz. can sweet corn, drained
- 1 14 oz. can fire-roasted diced tomatoes, drained
- 2 tablespoons taco seasoning
- 1 teaspoon smoked paprika
- 1/2 teaspoon coriander
- 1 cup fresh Pico de Gallo
- 6 flour tortillas, burrito size

Directions:
1. Set the air fryer to 400F/205C. Mix the shredded chicken, cream cheese, Mexican cheese, black beans, sweet corn, tomatoes, taco seasoning, smoked paprika, coriander, and Pico de Gallo in a large bowl.
2. Place 1 cup of the chicken burrito in the middle of each tortilla, then fold the sides of the tortilla over, and roll it up.

3. Mist the southwest chicken burrito with olive oil spray, then place it into the air fryer's basket.

4. Cook the southwest chicken burritos for 5 minutes, turn them over and cook for additional 5 minutes.

Nutrition: Calories: 698 Carbs: 83 g Fat: 26 g Protein: 34 g

43. Beef Bulgogi Burgers

Preparation time: 15 minutes

Cooking time: 10 minutes

Servings: 5

Ingredients:

For the Bulgogi Burgers:
- 1 lb. lean ground beef
- 2 tablespoons Korean red chili paste
- 1 tablespoon tamari
- 1 clove garlic, minced
- 1 tablespoon ginger, grated
- 1 tablespoon honey
- 1 tablespoon toasted sesame oil
- 1/4 cup shallots, chopped
- 1/2 teaspoon kosher salt

For the red chili mayonnaise:
- 2 tablespoons mayonnaise
- 2 tablespoons sour cream
- 1 tablespoon Korean red chili paste
- 4 hamburger buns for serving

Directions:
1. Combine the ground beef, Korean red chili paste, tamari, garlic, ginger, honey, sesame oil, shallots, and salt in a large bowl.
2. Let the beef bulgogi mixture marinate for 30 minutes or up overnight in the refrigerator.
3. Form the beef bulgogi mixture into four uniform patties and place them into the air fryer's basket.
4. Make an imprint with your thumb into the center of the burgers and cook them for 10 minutes at 360F/182C.
5. To make the red chili mayonnaise, whisk the mayonnaise, sour cream, and Korean red chili paste in a small bowl.
6. Slather the buns with the red chili mayonnaise and tip with the beef bulgogi burgers.

Nutrition: Calories: 334 Carbs: 12 g Fat: 21 g Protein: 25 g

44. Broccoli and Cheese Stuffed Chicken

Preparation time: 15 minutes
Cooking time: 20 minutes
Servings: 4
Ingredients:
- 2 cups finely chopped broccoli florets
- 8 thin chicken breast cutlets
- 1 large egg
- 2 teaspoons water
- 3/4 cup panko
- 4 slices cheddar cheese, cut in half
- 3/4 teaspoon kosher salt
- 1/2 teaspoon black pepper
- 1 teaspoon garlic powder
- 1 teaspoon onion powder

Directions:
1. Set your air fryer to 400F/205C, then spray a cookie sheet with nonstick cooking spray. Place broccoli into a bowl along with1 a tablespoon of water.
2. Cover the broccoli with water and heat it in the microwave for 1 minute until soft.

3. Whisk the large egg and water in a shallow baking dish until it is frothy, then place the breadcrumbs into a separate bowl.
4. Season the chicken cutlets with salt, pepper, garlic powder, and onion powder, then add 1/2 slice of cheddar cheese in the center of the chicken.
5. Add two tablespoons of the steamed broccoli, roll the chicken up to seal the filling, and then fasten it with toothpicks.
6. Dredge the stuffed chicken breast into the egg wash, then breadcrumbs, and place it onto a parchment-lined cookie sheet.
7. Mist, both sides of the broccoli cheese, stuffed chicken, then place it into the air fryer's basket.
8. Cook the broccoli and cheese stuffed chicken for 7-8 minutes, turn them over and cook for additional 7-8 minutes.

Nutrition: Calories: 270 Carbs: 22 g Fat: 6 g Protein: 17 g

45. Cajun Chicken Fried Steak Strips

Preparation Time: 10 minutes
Cooking time: 11 minutes
Servings: 8
Ingredients:
- 3 lbs. cube steaks
- 2/3 cups of all-purpose flour
- 1/2 teaspoon black pepper
- 1 teaspoon kosher salt
- 1 teaspoon smoked paprika
- 1 teaspoon garlic powder
- 1 teaspoon Cajun seasoning
- 1 cup of buttermilk
- 1 large egg
- 2 cups panko breadcrumbs

Directions:
1. Slice the cubed steak into strips before seasoning them with salt and pepper. Whisk the all-purpose flour, paprika, garlic powder, and Cajun seasoning in a small bowl.

2. Whisk the large egg and buttermilk in a separate shallow container. Place the panko breadcrumbs into another shallow baking dish.
3. Dredge the cube steaks into the seasoned flour, then into the egg and buttermilk mixture, and the breadcrumbs.
4. Place the chicken fried steak strips onto a parchment-lined baking sheet and let them sit for 10 minutes. Set the air fryer to 360F/182C.
5. Mist both sides of the cube steaks with olive oil spray and place them into the air fryer's basket in an even layer.
6. Cook the chicken fried steak for 7 minutes, then turn them over and cook for additional 3-4 minutes.

Nutrition: Calories: 280 Carbs: 10 g Fat: 14 g Protein: 27 g

46. Meatballs Sandwich

Preparation time: 10 minutes
Cooking time: 22 minutes
Servings: 4
Ingredients:
- 3 baguettes, sliced more than halfway through
- 14 ounces beef, ground
- 7 ounces tomato sauce
- 1 small onion, chopped
- 1 egg, whisked
- 1 tablespoon breadcrumbs
- 2 tablespoons cheddar cheese, grated
- 1 tablespoon oregano, chopped
- 1 tablespoon olive oil
- Salt and black pepper to the taste
- 1 teaspoon thyme, dried
- 1 teaspoon basil, dried

Directions:
1. In a bowl, combine meat with salt, pepper, onion, breadcrumbs, egg, cheese, oregano, thyme and basil, stir, shape medium meatballs and add them to your air fryer after you've greased it with the oil.

2. Cook them at 375F/191C for 12 minutes, flipping them halfway. Add tomato sauce, cook meatballs for 10 minutes more and arrange them on sliced baguettes. Serve them right away.

Nutrition: Calories 380 Fat 5 g Carbs 34 g Protein 20 g

47. Bacon Pudding

Preparation time: 10 minutes
Cooking time: 30 minutes
Servings: 6
Ingredients:
- 4 bacon strips, cooked and chopped
- 1 tablespoon butter, soft
- 2 cups corn
- 1 yellow onion, chopped
- ¼ cup celery, chopped
- ½ cup red bell pepper, chopped
- 1 teaspoon thyme, chopped
- 2 teaspoons garlic, minced
- Salt and black pepper to the taste
- ½ cup heavy cream
- 1 and ½ cups milk
- 3 eggs, whisked
- 3 cups bread, cubed
- 4 tablespoons parmesan, grated
- Cooking spray

Directions:
1. Grease your air fryer's pan with cooking spray.
2. In a bowl, mix bacon with butter, corn, onion, bell pepper, celery, thyme, garlic, salt, pepper, milk, heavy cream, eggs and bread cubes, toss, pour into greased pan and sprinkle cheese all over.
3. Add this to your preheated air fryer at 320F/160C and cook for 30 minutes. Divide among plates and serve warm for a quick lunch.

Nutrition: Calories 276 Fat 10 g Carbs 20 g Protein 10 g

48. Coconut and Chicken Casserole

Preparation time: 10 minutes

Cooking time: 25 minutes

Servings: 4

Ingredients:
- 4 lime leaves, torn
- 1 cup veggie stock
- 1 lemongrass stalk, chopped
- 1-inch piece, grated
- 1 pound chicken breast, skinless, boneless, and cut into thin strips
- 8 ounces mushrooms, chopped
- 4 Thai chilies, chopped
- 4 tablespoons fish sauce
- 6 ounces coconut milk
- ¼ cup lime juice
- ¼ cup cilantro, chopped
- Salt and black pepper to the taste

Directions:
1. Put the stock into a pan that fits your air fryer, bring to a simmer over medium heat, add lemongrass, ginger, and lime leaves, stir and cook for 10 minutes.
2. Strain soup, return to pan, add chicken, mushrooms, milk, chilies, fish sauce, lime juice, cilantro, salt, and pepper, stir, introduce in your air fryer and cook at 360F/182C for 15 minutes. Serve.

Nutrition: Calories 150 Fat 4 g Carbs 6 g Protein 7 g

49. Salmon and Asparagus

Preparation time: 10 minutes

Cooking time: 23 minutes

Servings: 4

Ingredients:
- 1 pound asparagus, trimmed

- 1 tablespoon olive oil
- A pinch of sweet paprika
- Salt and black pepper to the taste
- A pinch of garlic powder
- A pinch of cayenne pepper
- 1 red bell pepper, cut into halves
- 4 ounces smoked salmon

Directions:
1. Put asparagus spears and bell pepper on a lined baking sheet that fits your air fryer, add salt, pepper, garlic powder, paprika, olive oil, cayenne pepper, toss to coat,
2. Introduce in the fryer, cook at 390F/199C for 8 minutes, flip and cook for 8 minutes more.
3. Add salmon, cook for 5 minutes, more, divide everything between plates and serve.

Nutrition: Calories 90 Fat 1 g Carbs 1.2 g Protein 4 g

50. Chicken and Corn Casserole

Preparation time: 10 minutes
Cooking time: 30 minutes
Servings: 6
Ingredients:
- 1 cup clean chicken stock
- 2 teaspoons garlic powder
- Salt and black pepper to the taste
- 6 ounces canned coconut milk
- 1 and ½ cups green lentils
- 2 pounds chicken breasts, skinless, boneless, and cubed
- 1/3 cup cilantro, chopped
- 3 cups corn
- 3 handfuls spinach
- 3 green onions, chopped

Directions:

1. In a pan that fits your air fryer, mix stock with coconut milk, salt, pepper, garlic powder, chicken, and lentils.
2. Add corn, green onions, cilantro, and spinach, stir well, introduce in your air fryer and cook at 350F/177C for 30 minutes. Enjoy!

Nutrition: Calories 345 Fat 12 g Carbs 20 g Protein 44 g

51. Chicken and Zucchini Lunch Mix

Preparation time: 10 minutes

Cooking time: 20 minutes

Servings: 4

Ingredients:
- 4 zucchinis, cut with a spiralizer
- 1 pound chicken breasts, skinless, boneless, and cubed
- 2 garlic cloves, minced
- 1 teaspoon olive oil
- Salt and black pepper to the taste
- 2 cups cherry tomatoes, halved
- ½ cup almonds, chopped

For the pesto:
- 2 cups basil
- 2 cups kale, chopped
- 1 tablespoon lemon juice
- 1 garlic clove
- ¾ cup pine nuts
- ½ cup olive oil
- A pinch of salt

Directions:
1. In your food processor, mix basil with kale, lemon juice, garlic, pine nuts, oil and a pinch of salt, pulse well and leave aside.
2. Heat a pan that fits your air fryer with the oil over medium heat, add garlic, stir and cook for 1 minute.

3. Add chicken, salt, pepper, stir, almonds, zucchini noodles, garlic, cherry tomatoes and the pesto you've made at the beginning, stir gently.
4. Introduce in the preheated air fryer and cook at 360F/182C for 17 minutes. Divide among plates and serve for lunch.

Nutrition: Calories 344 Fat 8 g Carbs 12 g Protein 16 g

52. Chicken, Beans, Corn and Quinoa Casserole

Preparation time: 10 minutes
Cooking time: 30 minutes
Servings: 8
Ingredients:
- 1 cup quinoa, already cooked
- 3 cups chicken breast, cooked and shredded
- 14 ounces canned black beans
- 12 ounces corn
- ½ cup cilantro, chopped
- 6 kale leaves, chopped
- ½ cup green onions, chopped
- 1 cup clean tomato sauce
- 1 cup clean salsa
- 2 teaspoons chili powder
- 2 teaspoons cumin, ground
- 3 cups mozzarella cheese, shredded
- 1 tablespoon garlic powder
- Cooking spray
- 2 jalapeno peppers, chopped

Directions:
1. Spray a baking dish that fits your air fryer with cooking spray, add quinoa, chicken, black beans, corn, cilantro, kale, green onions, tomato sauce, salsa, chili powder, cumin, garlic powder, jalapenos and mozzarella, toss.
2. Introduce in your air fryer and cook at 350F/177c for 17 minutes. Slice and serve warm for lunch.

Nutrition: Calories 365 Fat 12 g Carbs 22 g Protein 26 g

53. Roly-Poly Air Fried White Fish

Preparation Time: 10 minutes

Cooking time: 10 minutes

Servings: 4

Ingredients:
- 4 lbs. of white fish fillets
- 2 ½ teaspoons of sea salt
- 4 mushrooms, sliced
- 1 teaspoon liquid stevia
- 2 tablespoons of Chinese winter pickle
- 2 tablespoons of vinegar
- 2 teaspoons chili powder
- 2 onions, thinly sliced
- 1 cup vegetable stock
- 2 tablespoons soy sauce

Directions:
1. Fill the fish fillets with mushrooms and pickles. Cut the onions into thinly sliced pieces. Spread the onions over the fish fillets.
2. Combine the stock, soy sauce, vinegar, sea salt, and stevia. Sprinkle the mixture over the fish fillets. Place the fish fillets into your air fryer and cook at 350F/177C for 10-minutes. Serve warm.

Nutrition: Calories: 278 Fat: 9.2 g Carbs: 7.4 g Protein: 33.2 g

54. Air Fried Dragon Shrimp

Preparation time: 10 minutes

Cooking time: 0 minutes

Servings: 2

Ingredients:
- ½ lb. shrimp

- ¼ cup almond flour
- Pinch of ginger
- 1 cup chopped green onions
- 2 tablespoons olive oil
- 2 eggs, beaten
- ½ cup soy sauce

Directions:
1. Boil the shrimps for 5-minutes. Prepare a paste made of ginger and onion. Now, beat the eggs, add the ginger paste, soya sauce and almond flour and combine well.
2. Add the shrimps to the mixture then place them in a baking dish and spray with oil. Cook shrimps at 390F/199C for 10-minutes.

Nutrition: Calories: 278 Fat: 8.6 g Carbs: 6.2 g Protein: 28.6 g

55. Coconut Lime Skirt Steak

Preparation time: 10 minutes
Cooking time: 25 minutes
Servings: 2
Ingredients:
- ½ cup coconut oil, melted

- Zest of one lime
- 2-1lb. grass-fed skirt steaks
- ¾ teaspoon sea salt
- 1 teaspoon red pepper flakes
- 1 teaspoon ginger, fresh, grated
- 1 tablespoon garlic, minced
- 2 tablespoons freshly squeezed lime juice

Directions:
1. In a mixing bowl, combine lime juice, coconut oil, garlic, ginger, red pepper, salt, and zest. Add the steaks and toss and rub with the marinade.
2. Allow the meat to marinate for about 20-minutes at room temperature. Transfer steaks to your air fryer directly on the rack. Cook steaks in the air fryer at 400F/205C for 5-minutes.

Nutrition: Calories: 312 Fat: 12.3 g Carbs: 6.4 g Protein: 42.1 g

56. Honey Sea Bass

Preparation time: 10 minutes
Cooking time: 10 minutes
Servings: 2
Ingredients:
- 2 sea bass fillets
- Zest from ½ orange, grated
- Juice from ½ orange
- A pinch of salt and black pepper
- 2 tablespoons mustard
- 2 teaspoons honey
- 2 tablespoons olive oil
- ½ pound canned lentils, drained
- A small bunch of dill, chopped
- 2 ounces watercress
- A small bunch of parsley, chopped

Directions:

1. Season fish fillets with salt and pepper, add orange zest and juice, rub with 1 tablespoon oil, with honey and mustard, rub, transfer to your air fryer and cook at 350F/177C for 10 minutes, flipping halfway.
2. Meanwhile, put lentils in a small pot, warm it up over medium heat, add the rest of the oil, watercress, dill, and parsley, stir well and divide among plates.
3. Add fish fillets and serve right away.

Nutrition: Calories 212 Fat 8 g Carbs 9 g Protein 17 g

57. Tuna Zucchini Melts

Preparation time: 15 minutes
Cooking time: 10 minutes
Servings: 4
Ingredients:
- 4 corn tortillas
- 3 tablespoons softened butter
- 1 (6-ounce) can chunk light tuna, drained
- 1 cup shredded zucchini, drained by squeezing in a kitchen towel
- 1/3 cup mayonnaise
- 2 tablespoons mustard
- 1 cup shredded Cheddar or Colby cheese

Directions:
1. Spread the tortillas with softened butter. Place in the air fryer basket and grill for 2 to 3 minutes or until the tortillas are crisp. Remove from basket and set aside.
2. In a medium bowl, combine the tuna, zucchini, mayonnaise, and mustard, and mix well.
3. Divide the tuna mixture among the toasted tortillas. Top each with some of the shredded cheese.
4. Grill in the air fryer for 2 to 4 minutes or until the tuna mixture is hot, and the cheese melts and starts to brown. Serve.

Nutrition: Calories: 428 Fat: 30 g Carbohydrates: 19 g Protein: 2 2g

58. Crispy Salt and Pepper Tofu

Preparation time: 5 minutes

Cooking time: 15 minutes

Servings: 4

Ingredients:
- ¼ cup chickpea flour
- ¼ cup arrowroot (or cornstarch)
- 1 teaspoon sea salt
- 1 teaspoon granulated garlic
- ½ teaspoon freshly grated black pepper
- 1 (15-ounce) package tofu, firm, or extra-firm
- Cooking oil spray (sunflower, safflower, or refined coconut)
- Asian Spicy Sweet Sauce, optional

Directions:
1. In a medium bowl, combine the flour, arrowroot, salt, garlic, and pepper. Stir well to combine.
2. Cut the tofu into cubes. Place the cubes into the flour mixture. Toss well to coat. Spray the tofu with oil and toss again.
3. Spray the air fryer basket with the oil. Place the tofu in a single layer in the air fryer basket and spray the tops with oil. Fry for 8 minutes.
4. Remove the air fryer basket and spray again with oil. Toss gently or turn the pieces over. Spray with oil again and fry for another 7 minutes, or until golden-browned and very crisp.
5. Serve immediately, either plain or with the Asian Spicy Sweet Sauce.

Nutrition: Calories: 148 Fat: 5 g Carbohydrates: 14 g Protein: 11 g

59. Garlic Herb Butter Chicken Wings

Preparation time: 15 minutes

Cooking time: 25 minutes

Servings: 3

Ingredients:
- 1 lb. chicken wings

- 1 teaspoon salt
- 1/2 teaspoon black pepper
- 1 teaspoon onion powder
- ¼ cup butter
- 2 cloves garlic, minced
- 1 teaspoon smoked paprika
- 2 tablespoons freshly minced parsley

Directions:
1. Season the wings with salt, pepper, and onion powder and place them into the air fryer's basket in an even layer.
2. Cook the garlic butter chicken wings for 10 minutes at 400F/205C. Turn the chicken wings over and cook them for another 10 minutes.
3. Add the butter and garlic to a small pot and heat it over medium-low heat until it is fragrant.
4. Remove the garlic-infused butter mixture from the heat and allow it to cool slightly before stirring in the smoked paprika and parsley.
5. Add the garlic butter chicken wings to a bowl and toss with garlic butter mixture.

Nutrition: Calories: 201 Carbs: 2 g Fat: 13 g Protein: 20 g

60. Beef Satay

Preparation time: 20 minutes
Cooking time: 16 minutes
Servings: 2-3

Ingredients:
- 1 lb. flank steak, thinly sliced into long strips
- 2 tablespoons olive oil
- 1 tablespoon oyster sauce
- 1 tablespoon soy sauce
- 2 tablespoons raw ginger, grated
- 2 cloves garlic, minced
- 1 tablespoon brown sugar
- 1 teaspoon cumin

- 1/2 cup chopped parsley, divided

Directions:
1. Whisk the olive oil, oyster sauce, soy sauce, ginger, garlic, brown sugar, cumin, and 1/4 cup parsley in a bowl, then add the beef and toss to coat.
2. Let the beef satay marinate for 30 minutes or overnight in the fridge. Place the beef satay into the air fryer's basket in an even layer and toss the marinade.
3. Cook the beef satay for 4 minutes at 400F/205C, then turn it over and cook for additional 4 minutes.
4. Set your air fryer to 400F/205C for 8 minutes, flipping once halfway.

Nutrition: Calories: 163 Carbs: 8 g Fat: 12 g Protein: 9 g

DINNER

61. Spicy Catfish

Preparation time: 5 minutes
Cooking time: 15 minutes
Servings: 4
Ingredients:
- 2 tbsp. cornmeal polenta
- 2 tsp. Cajun seasoning

- ½ tsp. paprika
- ½ tsp. garlic powder
- Salt, as required
- 2 (6-oz) catfish fillets
- 1 tbsp. olive oil

Directions:

1. In a container, mix together the cornmeal, Cajun seasoning, paprika, garlic powder, and salt. Add the catfish fillets and coat evenly with the mixture. Now, coat each fillet with oil.
2. Arrange the fish fillets onto a greased cooking rack and spray with cooking spray. Arrange the drip pan in the bottom of the Instant Vortex Air Fryer Oven cooking chamber. Select "Air Fry" and then adjust the temperature to 400 °F. Set the timer for 14 minutes and press "Start."
3. When the display shows "Add Food," insert the cooking rack in the center position, the display shows "Turn Food" turn the fillets.
4. Remove the rack from the Vortex Oven when the cooking time is complete. Serve hot.

Nutrition: Calories: 32 Carbs: 6.7 g Fat: 20.3 g Protein: 27.3 g

62. BBQ Chicken Recipe from Greece

Preparation time: 5 minutes

Cooking time: 24minutes

Servings: 2

Ingredients:

- 1 (8 ounces) container fat-free plain yogurt
- 2 tbsp. fresh lemon juice
- 2 tsp. dried oregano
- 1-pound skinless, boneless chicken breast halves - cut into 1-inch pieces
- 1 large red onion, cut into wedges
- 1/2 tsp. lemon zest
- 1/2 tsp. salt
- 1 large green bell pepper, cut into 1 1/2-inch piece
- 1/3 cup crumbled feta cheese with basil and sun-dried tomatoes
- 1/4 tsp. ground black pepper

- 1/4 tsp. crushed dried rosemary

Directions:
1. In a shallow dish, mix well rosemary, pepper, salt, oregano, lemon juice, lemon zest, feta cheese, and yogurt. Add chicken and toss well to coat. Marinate in the ref for 3 hours.
2. Thread bell pepper, onion, and chicken pieces in skewers. Place on skewer rack.
3. For 12 minutes, cook it on 360oF. Turnover skewers halfway through cooking time. If needed, cook in batches.
4. Serve and enjoy.

Nutrition: Calories: 242 Carbs: 12.3 g Protein: 31.0 g Fat: 7.5 g

63. Juicy Cheeseburgers

Preparation time: 5 minutes
Cooking time: 15 minutes
Servings: 4
Ingredients:
- 1 pound 93% lean ground beef
- 1 tsp. Worcestershire sauce
- 1 tbsp. burger seasoning
- Salt to taste
- Pepper to taste
- Cooking oil
- 4 slices cheese
- Buns

Directions:
1. Mix in a large container the ground beef, Worcestershire, burger seasoning, salt, and pepper to taste until well blended. Spray the cooking basket with cooking oil. You will need only a quick spirit. The burgers will produce oil as they cook. Shape the mixture into 4 patties. Place the burgers in the air fryer. The burgers should fit without the need to stack, but stacking is okay if necessary.
2. Pour into the Oven rack/basket. Place the Rack on the middle-shelf of the Air Fryer Oven. Set temperature to 375°F, and set time to 8 minutes. Cook for 8 minutes. Open the air fryer and turnover

the burgers. Then, cook further for about 3 to 4 minutes. Check the inner portion of the burgers to determine if they have finished cooking. You can use a knife or fork to examine the color in the center.
3. Top each burger with a slice of cheese. Cook for an extra minute, or until the cheese has melted
4. Serve on buns with any additional toppings of your choice.

Nutrition: Calories: 566 Fat: 39 g Carbs: 0 g Protein: 29 g

64. Warming Winter Beef with Celery

Preparation time: 5 minutes
Cooking time: 12 minutes
Servings: 4
Ingredients:
- 9 ounces tender beef, chopped
- 1/2 cup leeks, chopped
- 1/2 cup celery stalks, chopped
- 2 cloves garlic, smashed
- 2 tbsp. red cooking wine
- 3/4 cup cream of celery soup
- 1/4 tsp. black pepper
- 1/4 tsp. smoked paprika
- 3/4 tsp. salt
- 2 sprigs rosemary, chopped

Directions:
1. Add the beef, leeks, celery, and garlic to the baking dish; cook for about 5 minutes at 390 degrees F.
2. Once the meat is starting to tender, pour in the wine and soup. Season with rosemary, smoked paprika, salt, and black pepper.
3. Now, cook an additional 7 minutes.

Nutrition: Calories: 364 Fat: 9 g Carbs: 39 g Protein: 32 g

65. Air Fryer Vegetables

Preparation time: 5 minutes

Cooking time: 10 minutes

Servings: 4

Ingredients:

- 1/2 lb. broccoli fresh
- 1/2 lb. cauliflower fresh
- 1 tbsp. Olive oil
- 1/4 tsp. seasoning
- 1/3 c water

Directions:

1. Mix vegetables, olive oil, and seasonings in a medium bowl.
2. Pour 1/3 c. water in the Air Fryer base to prevent smoking.
3. Place vegetables in the air fryer basket.
4. Cook at 400 degrees for 7-10 minutes.
5. Shake vegetables halfway through the 7-10 minutes.

Nutrition: Calories: 65 Carbs: 7 g Protein: 3 g Fat: 4 g

66. Pork Meatballs

Preparation time: 10 minutes

Cooking time: 20 minutes

Servings: 4

Ingredients:

- 12 ounces ground pork
- 1/2 cup panko bread crumbs
- 1 egg
- 1 tsp. salt
- 1 tsp. dried parsley
- 1/2 tsp. paprika

Directions:

1. Preheat the air fryer oven to 175 ° C. Mix ground pork, panko breadcrumbs, eggs, salt, parsley, and paprika in a large bowl and mix well.
2. Make 12 large meatballs with a scoop of ice cream.
3. On a baking sheet, place half of the meatballs in the basket and cook for 8 minutes.
4. Shake the basket and cook for another 2 minutes Place on a serving plate and let rest for 5 minutes. Repeat with the remaining meatballs.

Nutrition: Calories: 64 Fat: 1.6 g Carbs: 3.3 g Protein: 8.5 g

67. Wondrous Creole Fried Shrimp with Sriracha Sauce

Preparation time: 10 minutes

Cooking time: 10 minutes

Servings: 4

Ingredients:

- 1 pound peeled and deveined shrimp
- ½ cup cornmeal
- ½ cup breadcrumbs
- 1 beaten egg
- 1 tbsp. hot sauce
- 1 tbsp. mustard
- 2 tbsp. creole seasoning
- 1 tsp. onion powder
- 1 tsp. garlic powder
- 1 tsp. black pepper
- 1 tsp. salt

Siracha sauce ingredients
- 1 cup mayonnaise
- 3 tbsp. sriracha sauce
- 1 tbsp. soy sauce
- 1 tsp. black pepper

Directions:
1. Turn on your air fryer to 360 degrees Fahrenheit.
2. Using a container, add the eggs, hot sauce, mustard, 1 tbsp of creole seasoning, onion powder, garlic powder, black pepper, salt, the shrimp, and toss adequately covered.
3. Using another bowl, add the breadcrumbs, flour, 1 tbsp of creole seasoning, and the shrimp and cover it adequately.
4. Grease your air fryer basket with a nonstick cooking spray and add the shrimp.
5. Cook it for 5 minutes or until it has a golden-brown color while being careful not to overcook.
6. After that, carefully remove it from your air fryer and allow it to cool.
7. Pick a separate bowl, add and mix all the sauce ingredients properly. Serve!

Nutrition: Calories: 200 Fat: 12 g Protein: 15 g Carbs: 7 g

68. Sesame Seeds Coated Fish

Preparation time: 20 minutes
Cooking time: 20 minutes
Servings: 28
Ingredients:
- ½ cup sesame seeds, toasted
- ½ tsp. dried rosemary, crushed
- 8 tbsp. olive oil
- 14 frozen fish fillets (white fish of your choice)
- 6 eggs and freshly ground black pepper
- ½ cup breadcrumbs
- 8 tbsp. plain flour
- Salt to taste

Directions:

1. Take three dishes, place flour in one, crack eggs in the other and mix remaining ingredients except for fillets in the third one.
2. Now, coat fillets in the flour and dip in the beaten eggs.
3. Then, dredge generously with the sesame seeds mixture.
4. Meanwhile, preheat the air fryer to 390 degrees F and line the air fryer basket with the foil.
5. Arrange fillets in the basket and cook for about 14 minutes, flipping once in a middle way.
6. Take out and serve hot.

Nutrition: Calories: 179 Fat: 9.3 g Carbs: 15.8 g Protein: 7.7 g

69. Brine-Soaked Turkey

Preparation time: 10 minutes

Cooking time: 45 minutes

Servings: 8

Ingredients:

- 7 lb. bone-in, skin-on turkey breast

Brine:

- 1/2 cup salt
- 1 lemon
- 1/2 onion
- 3 cloves garlic, smashed
- 5 sprigs fresh thyme
- 3 bay leaves
- Black pepper to taste

Turkey Breast:

- 4 tbsp. butter, softened
- 1/2 tsp. black pepper
- 1/2 tsp. garlic powder
- 1/4 tsp. dried thyme
- 1/4 tsp. dried oregano

Directions:

1. Mix the turkey brine ingredients in a pot and soak the turkey in the brine overnight. The next day, remove the soaked turkey from the brine.
2. Whisk the butter, black pepper, garlic powder, oregano, and thyme. Brush the butter mixture over the turkey, then place it in a baking tray.
3. Press the "Power Button" of Air Fry Oven and turn the dial to select the "Air Roast" mode. Press the Time button and again turn the dial to set the cooking time to 45 minutes.
4. Now, push the Temp button and rotate the dial to set the temperature at 370 degrees F. Once preheated, place the turkey baking tray in the oven and close its lid.
5. Slice and serve warm.

Nutrition: Calories: 397 Fat: 15.4 g Carbs: 58.5 g Protein: 7.9 g

70. Miso Glazed Salmon

Preparation time: 5 minutes
Cooking time: 10 minutes
Servings: 4
Ingredients:
- 1/3 cup's sake
- ¼ cup sugar
- ¼ cup red miso
- 1 tbsp. low-sodium soy sauce
- 2 tbsp. vegetable oil
- 4 (5-oz) skinless salmon fillets, (1-inch thick)

Directions:
1. Place the sake, sugar, miso, soy sauce, and oil into a bowl and beat until thoroughly combined. Rub the salmon fillets with the mixture generously. In a plastic zip-lock bag, place the salmon fillets with any remaining miso mixture.
2. Seal the bag and refrigerate to marinate for about 30 minutes. Grease a baking dish that will fit in the Vortex Air Fryer Oven. Remove the salmon fillets from the bag and shake off the excess marinade. Arrange the salmon fillets into the prepared baking dish.
3. Arrange the drip pan in the bottom of the Instant Vortex Air Fryer Oven cooking chamber. Select "Broil" and set the time for 5 minutes.

4. When the display shows "Add Food," insert the baking dish in the center position.
5. When the display shows "Turn Food," do not turn the food. When cooking time is complete, remove the baking dish from the Vortex Oven. Serve hot.

Nutrition: Calories: 335 Carbs: 18.3 g Fat: 16.6 g Protein: 29.8 g

71. Lemon Chicken Breasts

Preparation time: 10 minutes
Cooking time: 30 minutes
Servings: 4
Ingredients:
- 1/4 cup olive oil
- 3 tbsp. garlic, minced
- 1/3 cup dry white wine
- 1 tbsp. lemon zest, grated
- 2 tbsp. lemon juice
- 1 1/2 tsp. dried oregano, crushed
- 1 tsp. thyme leaves, minced
- Salt and black pepper
- 4 skin-on boneless chicken breasts
- 1 lemon, sliced

Directions:
1. Whisk everything in a baking pan to coat the chicken breasts well.
2. Place the lemon slices on top of the chicken breasts.
3. Spread the mustard mixture over the toasted bread slices.
4. Press the "Power Button" of Air Fry Oven and turn the dial to select the "Bake" mode.
5. Press the Time button and again turn the dial to set the cooking time to 30 minutes.
6. Now push the Temp button and rotate the dial to set the temperature at 370 degrees F.
7. Once preheated, place the baking pan inside and close its lid.
8. Serve warm.

Nutrition: Calories: 388 Fat: 8 g Carbs: 8 g Protein: 13 g

72. Breaded Cod

Preparation time: 5 minutes

Cooking time: 10 minutes

Servings: 4

Ingredients:
- 1/3 cup all-purpose flour
- Ground black pepper, as required
- 1 large egg
- 2 tbsp. water
- 2/3 cup cornflakes, crushed
- 1 tbsp. parmesan cheese, grated
- 1/8 tsp. cayenne pepper
- 1 lb. Cod fillets
- Salt to taste

Directions:
1. In a shallow bowl, add the flour and black pepper and mix well. In a second shallow dish, add the egg and water and beat well. In a third shallow dish, add the cornflakes, cheese, and cayenne pepper and mix well.
2. Season the cod fillets with salt evenly. Coat the fillets with flour mixture, then dip into the egg mixture and finally coat with the cornflake mixture.
3. Arrange the cod fillets onto the greased cooking rack. Arrange the drip pan in the bottom of the Instant Vortex Air Fryer Oven cooking chamber. Select "Air Fry" and then adjust the temperature to 400 °F. Set the time for 10 minutes and push the "Start" button.
4. When the display shows "Add Food," insert the cooking rack in the bottom position, the display shows "Turn Food" turn the cod fillets. When cooking time is complete, remove the tray from the Vortex Oven. Serve hot.

Nutrition: Calories: 168 Carbs: 12.1 g Fat: 2.7 g Protein: 23.7 g

73. Basil-Garlic Breaded Chicken Bake

Preparation time: 5 minutes

Cooking time: 30 minutes

Servings: 2

Ingredients:

- 2 halves boneless skinless chicken breast (4 ounces each)
- 1 tbsp. butter, melted
- 1 large tomato, seeded and chopped
- 2 garlic cloves, minced
- 1 1/2 tbsp. minced fresh basil
- 1/2 tbsp. olive oil
- 1/2 tsp. salt
- 1/4 cup all-purpose flour
- 1/4 cup egg substitute
- 1/4 cup grated Parmesan cheese
- 1/4 cup dry bread crumbs
- 1/4 tsp. pepper

Directions:

1. In a shallow container, whisk the egg substitute and place flour in a separate bowl. Incline the chicken in flour, then the egg mix, and finally the flour. In a small bowl, whisk well the butter, bread crumbs, and cheese. Sprinkle over chicken.
2. Lightly grease the baking pan of the air fryer with cooking spray. Place breaded chicken on the bottom of the pan. Cover with foil.
3. For 20 minutes, cook it at 390 F.
4. Meanwhile, in a bowl, whisk well-remaining ingredients.
5. Remove foil from pan and then pour over chicken the remaining Ingredients—Cook for 8 minutes. Serve and enjoy.

Nutrition: Calories: 311 Carbs: 22.0 g Protein: 31.0 g Fat: 11.0 g

74. Cheeseburger Egg Rolls

Preparation time: 10 minutes

Cooking time: 7 minutes

Servings: 6

Ingredients:
- 6 egg roll wrappers
- 6 chopped dill pickle chips
- 1 tbsp. yellow mustard
- 3 tbsp. cream cheese
- 3 tbsp. shredded cheddar cheese
- ½ C. chopped onion
- ½ C. chopped bell pepper
- ¼ tsp. onion powder
- ¼ tsp. garlic powder
- 8 ounces of raw lean ground beef

Directions:
1. In a skillet, add seasonings, beef, onion, and bell pepper. Stir and crumble beef till fully cooked and vegetables are soft.
2. Take the frypan off the heat and add cream cheese, mustard, and cheddar cheese, stirring till melted.
3. Pour beef mixture into a bowl and fold in pickles.
4. Layout egg wrappers and place 1/6th of beef mixture into each one. Moisten egg roll wrapper edges with water. Fold sides to the middle and seal with water.
5. Repeat with all other egg rolls.
6. Place rolls into the air fryer, one batch at a time.
7. Pour into the Oven rack/basket. Place the Rack on the middle-shelf of the Air Fryer Oven. Set temperature to 392°F, and set time to 7 minutes

Nutrition: Calories: 153 Fat: 4 g Carbs: 0 g Protein: 12 g

75. Creamy Burger and Potato Bake

Preparation time: 5 minutes
Cooking time: 55 minutes
Servings: 3
Ingredients:
- Salt to taste
- Freshly ground pepper, to taste

- 1/2 (10.75 ounces) can condense cream of mushroom soup
- 1/2-pound lean ground beef
- 1-1/2 cups peeled and thinly sliced potatoes
- 1/2 cup shredded Cheddar cheese
- 1/4 cup chopped onion
- 1/4 cup and 2 tbsp. milk

Directions:

1. Lightly grease the baking pan of the air fryer with cooking spray. Add ground beef. For 10 minutes, cook on 360°F.
2. Stir and crumble halfway through cooking time.
3. Meanwhile, in a bowl, whisk well pepper, salt, milk, onion, and mushroom soup. Mix well.
4. Dry out fat off ground beef and transfer beef to a plate.
5. In the same air fryer baking pan, layer ½ of potatoes on the bottom, then ½ of soup mixture, and then ½ of beef. Repeat process.
6. Cover pans with foil.
7. Cook for 30 minutes. Remove foil and cook until potatoes are tender for an additional 15 minutes.
8. Serve and enjoy.

Nutrition: Calories: 399 Fat: 26.9 g Carbs: 0 g Protein: 22.1 g

76. Roasted Heirloom Tomato with Baked Feta

Preparation time: 20 minutes

Cooking time: 14 minutes

Servings: 2

Ingredients:

- 1 ea. Heirloom tomato
- 8 oz. Feta cheese block
- ½ cup red onions (sliced paper-thin)
- 1 tbsp. Olive oil

For Basil Pesto:

- ½ cup parsley (rough chopped)
- ½ cup basil (rough chopped)

- ½ cup parmesan (freshly grated)
- 3 tbsp. toasted pine nuts
- 1 ea. Garlic clove
- ½ cup olive oil
- 1 pinch salt

Directions:
1. First, preheat the Air fryer to 390°F.
2. Combine pine nuts, 1 tsp: olive oil, and a pinch of salt.
3. Toss pine nuts into the Air fryer and set the timer for 2 minutes. Remove and place onto a paper towel and set aside.
4. Wash and chop one bunch of parsley and one bunch of basil.
5. Place chopped parsley, basil, freshly grated parmesan, garlic, toasted pine nuts, and salt in a small pot over medium-high heat.
6. Turn on the food processor and drizzle within the olive oil.
7. Remove the pesto and refrigerate.
8. Slice the tomato into ½ inch thick slices. Slice the feta into ½ inch thick slices. Then, cut the feta the same size as the heirloom tomato with a circle cutter.
9. Mass the feta on top of the tomato and spread 1 tbsp basil pesto in between.
10. Slice the red onions paper-thin and toss with 1 tbsp of olive oil and apply to the feta's top.
11. Place tomatoes into the air fryer and cook for 12-14 minutes.
12. Finish with sea salt and basil pesto.

Nutrition: Calories: 322.2 Fat: 30.8 g Carbs: 7.7 g Protein: 32 g

77. Stevia -Cajun Chicken Thighs

Preparation time: 10 minutes
Cooking time: 25 minutes
Servings: 4
Ingredients:
- 1 ½ pounds skinless, boneless chicken thighs
- ¼ cup coconut flour
- 1/3 cup almond flour

- 2 ½ tsp. Cajun seasoning
- ½ tsp. garlic powder
- ½ tsp. stevia powder
- ¼ tsp. ground paprika
- 1/8 tsp. cayenne pepper
- ¼ tsp. salt

Directions:

1. Mix coconut flour, almond flour, Cajun spice, garlic powder, salt, stevia powder, paprika, and cayenne pepper in a dish. The thighs distribute the flour mixture. Remove extra flour.
2. Preheat a deep fryer to 175 °C (360 degrees F). Place the chicken legs in the frying basket and let them done within 15 minutes. Turn the legs over until the chicken legs in the middle are no longer pink, and the juice comes out clearly for about 10 minutes longer.
3. A quick reading thermometer in the middle should show at least 74 ° C (165 ° F). Take the chicken legs out of the deep fryer and sprinkle the lemon juice over each leg.

Nutrition: Calories: 121 Fat: 9.1 g Carbs: 3.3 g Protein: 7.2 g

78. Chicken Cordon Bleu

Preparation time: 60 minutes
Cooking time: 40 minutes
Servings: 6
Ingredients:
- 1 garlic clove
- 2 eggs
- 2 tsp. butter, melted

- 1 cup bread, ground
- 0.25 cup flour
- 2 tsp. fresh thyme
- 16 slices Swiss cheese
- 8 slices ham
- 4 chicken breasts

Directions:

1. Turn on the air fryer to heat to 350 degrees.
2. Flatten out the chicken and then fill with two slices of cheese, ham, and then cheese again. Roll up and use a toothpick to keep together.
3. Mix the garlic, thyme, and bread together with the butter. Then, beat the eggs and season the flour with pepper and salt.
4. Pass the chicken rolls through the flour, then the egg, and then the breadcrumbs. Add to the air fryer to cook.
5. After 20 minutes, take the chicken out and cool down before serving.

Nutrition: Calories: 387 Carbs: 18 g Fat: 20 g Protein: 33 g

79. Chicken Drumsticks

Preparation time: 10 minutes
Cooking time: 20 minutes
Servings: 8
Ingredients:

- 8 chicken drumsticks
- 2 tbsp. olive oil
- 1 tsp. salt
- 1 tsp. pepper
- 1 tsp. garlic powder
- 1 tsp. paprika
- 1/2 tsp. cumin

Directions:

1. Mix olive oil with salt, black pepper, garlic powder, paprika, and cumin in a bowl.

2. Rub this mixture liberally over all the drumsticks.
3. Place these drumsticks in the air fryer basket.
4. Turn the dial to select the "Air Fry" mode.
5. Hit the Time button and again use the dial to set the cooking time to 20 minutes.
6. Now push the Temp button and rotate the dial to set the temperature at 375 degrees F.
7. Once preheated, place the Air fryer basket inside the oven.
8. Flip the drumsticks when cooked halfway through.
9. Resume air frying for another rest of the 10 minutes.
10. Serve warm.

Nutrition: Calories: 212 Fat: 11.8 g Carbs: 14.6 g Protein: 17.3 g

80. Cajun Salmon

Preparation time: 5 minutes

Cooking time: 10 minutes

Servings: 2

Ingredients:

- 2 Salmon steaks
- 2 tbsp. Cajun seasoning

Directions:

1. Rub the salmon steaks with the Cajun seasoning evenly. Set aside for about 10 minutes. Arrange the salmon steaks onto the greased cooking tray.
2. Arrange the drip pan in the bottom of the Instant Vortex Air Fryer Oven cooking chamber. Select "Air Fry" and then adjust the temperature to 390 °F. Set the air fryer time to 8 minutes and press "Start."
3. When the display shows "Add Food," insert the cooking tray in the center position. When the display shows "Turn Food," turn the salmon steaks.
4. When the timer stops, remove the tray from the Vortex Oven. Serve hot.

Nutrition: Calories: 225 Carbs: 0 g Fat: 10.5 g Protein: 22.1 g

81. Pistachio-Crusted Chicken Breast

Preparation time: 10 minutes

Cooking time: 15-18 minutes

Servings: 2-3

Ingredients:
- 2 6 oz. boneless, skinless chicken breast
- 1/2 teaspoon sea salt
- 1/2 teaspoon black pepper
- teaspoon smoked paprika
- 1 teaspoon fresh thyme, chopped
- 1 teaspoon fresh rosemary, chopped
- 2 tablespoons mayonnaise
- 1/2 cup pistachios, crushed

Directions:
1. Season the chicken breasts with sea salt, black pepper, and smoked paprika. Whisk the mayonnaise, rosemary, and thyme in a small bowl.
2. Slather the mayonnaise herb mixture on top of both chicken breasts, then top them with the crushed pistachios.
3. Place the pistachio-crusted chicken breast into the air fryer's basket and mist the tops with olive oil spray. Cook the pistachio-crusted chicken breast 370F/188C for 15-18 minutes.

Nutrition: Calories: 175 Carbs: 6 g Fat: 6 g Protein: 28 g

82. Garlic Lemon Pepper Scallops

Preparation time: 10 minutes

Cooking time: 4-5 minutes

Servings: 3

Ingredients:
- 1 lb. scallops
- 2 tablespoons butter, melted
- 1 tablespoon minced garlic

- 1 teaspoon kosher salt
- 1 teaspoon freshly chopped parsley
- 1 teaspoon chopped chives
- 1 1/2 teaspoons lemon pepper
- 1 teaspoon lemon juice

Directions:
1. Pat your scallops dry with paper towels, then set them aside. Set your air fryer to 400F/205C.
2. Whisk the melted butter, garlic, salt, parsley, chives, lemon pepper, and lemon juice in a bowl. Mist the air fryer's basket with nonstick cooking spray.
3. Brush the scallops with the garlic lemon pepper butter and place them into the air fryer's basket.
4. Cook the garlic lemon pepper scallops for 5 minutes, turn them over and cook for another 4-5 minutes. Serve.

Nutrition: Calories: 90 Carbs: 3 g Fat: 2 g Protein: 13 g

83. Chili Lime Chicken Thighs

Preparation time: 10 minutes

Cooking time: 26 minutes

Servings: 4

Ingredients:
- 4 bone-in chicken thighs
- 2 tablespoons lime juice
- 2 tablespoons olive oil
- 1 tablespoon ancho chili powder
- 1 teaspoon seasoned salt
- 1/2 teaspoon black pepper
- 1 teaspoon smoked paprika
- 1 teaspoon garlic powder

Directions:
1. Whisk the lime juice, olive oil, ancho chili powder, seasoned salt, black pepper, smoked paprika, and garlic powder in a bowl.
2. Add the chicken thighs to the bowl and toss to coat the meat in the chili lime seasoning.

3. Mist the air fryer's basket with olive oil spray, then add the chicken thighs to the basket skin side down.
4. Mist the chicken thighs with olive oil spray and cook the chicken thighs for 10 minutes at 350F/177C.
5. Turn the chicken thighs over and cook them for an additional 10 minutes until it reaches a temperature of 165F/74C.
6. Increase the air fryer's temperature to 400F/205C and cook for 3-6 minutes until the skin is crispy.

Nutrition: Calories: 110 Carbs: 3 g Fat: 3 g Protein: 18 g

84. Spicy Lime Flank Steak

Preparation time: 10 minutes
Cooking time: 12 minutes
Servings: 5
Ingredients:
- 1 lb. flank steak
- zest and juice of 1 lime
- 1 jalapeno, minced
- 3 cloves of garlic, minced
- 1/2 cup fresh cilantro, minced
- 2 tablespoons honey
- 1 teaspoon paprika
- 1/2 teaspoon chili powder
- 1/2 teaspoon black pepper
- 1 teaspoon kosher salt
- 1/4 cup olive oil

Directions:
1. Program your air fryer to 400F/205C. Whisk lime zest, lime juice, jalapeno, garlic, cilantro, honey, chili powder, pepper, and salt in a shallow dish.
2. Toss the flank steak in the marinade and allow it to sit for 30 minutes. Place the flank steak into the air fryer's basket and cook for 10 minutes.
3. Turn the flank steak over and cook for another 1-2 minutes until it reaches your preferred temperature.
4. Let the spicy lime flank steak cook for at least 10 minutes before slicing.

Nutrition: Calories: 554 Carbs: 8 g Fat: 0 g Protein: 53 g

85. Mustard-Glazed Pork Tenderloin

Preparation time: 10 minutes
Cooking time: 15-20 minutes
Servings: 4
Ingredients:
- 1 1/2 lb. pork tenderloin, rinsed, dried
- 2 cloves garlic, minced
- 1/4 teaspoon kosher salt
- 1/2 teaspoon black pepper
- 1 teaspoon onion powder
- 1/4 cup Dijon mustard
- 1/4 cup maple syrup
- 1 teaspoon herb de Provence
- 1 teaspoon dried thyme

Directions:
1. Cut a few shallow crevices into the pork loin and stuff it with the minced garlic. Generously season the pork tenderloin with salt, pepper, and onion powder.
2. Whisk the Dijon mustard, herb de Provence, and thyme in a bowl.
3. Slather the mustard glaze or the entire pork tenderloin, place it in a container, cover it with plastic wrap and marinate it for 2-3 hours.
4. Cook the mustard glazed pork tenderloin for 15-20 minutes at 400F/205C until it reaches a temperature of 145F/63C.
5. Allow the mustard-glazed pork tenderloin to sit for 5 minutes before carving.

Nutrition: Calories: 237 Carbs: 7 g Fat: 6 g Protein: 35 g

86. Roasted Turkey Legs

Preparation time: 15 minutes
Cooking time: 40 minutes

Servings: 2-3

Ingredients:
- 1 1/2 teaspoons smoked paprika
- 1 teaspoon brown sugar
- 1 teaspoon kosher salt
- 1 teaspoon garlic powder
- 1 teaspoon onion powder
- 1/2 teaspoon cayenne pepper
- 1 teaspoon oregano
- 2 large turkey legs

Directions:
1. Whisk the smoked paprika, brown sugar, salt, garlic powder, onion powder, cayenne pepper, and oregano in a small bowl.
2. Rinse the turkey legs with cold water, then pat dry with turkey legs.
3. Massage the seasoning mixture over turkey legs, being sure to get the seasoning underneath the skin.
4. Place the turkey legs into the air fryer's basket and mist them with olive oil spray.
5. Cook the turkey legs for 20 minutes at 400F/205C, turn them over and cook for additional 20 minutes.

Nutrition: Calories: 170 Carbs: 0 g Fat: 5 g Protein: 29 g

DESSERT

87. French Style Yogurt Treat

Preparation time: 8-10 minutes
Cooking time: 6 minutes
Servings: 4-5
Ingredients:
- 1 teaspoon vanilla extract
- 2 eggs, large
- 2 slices sourdough bread
- Butter as needed
- 1 to 2 teaspoon squeeze honey
- Greek yogurt for serving
- Your favorite choice of berries

Directions:
1. Place your air fryer on a flat kitchen surface; plug it and turn it on. Set temperature to 355 degrees F and let it preheat for 4-5 minutes.
2. Take out the air-frying basket and gently coat it using a cooking oil or spray.
3. In a bowl of medium size, thoroughly whisk the vanilla and eggs. Take the bread slices and spread butter on their every side. Soak them with the egg mix.
4. Add the slices to the basket. Push the air-frying basket in the air fryer. Cook for 3 minutes.
5. Slide out the basket; serve warm!
6. Top them with the yogurt honey and berries!

Nutrition: Calories: 77 Fat: 2 g Carbohydrates: 10 g Fiber: 0 g Protein: 4 g

88. Pineapple Cinnamon Treat

Preparation time: 8-10 minutes

Cooking time: 8 minutes

Servings: 6

Ingredients:
- 1/2 teaspoon baking soda
- 1/2 teaspoon ground cinnamon
- 1/4 teaspoon ground anise star
- 1/4 cup flaked coconut, unsweetened
- 1 pineapple, sliced
- A pinch of kosher salt
- 1/2 cup water
- 2/3 cup all-purpose flour
- 1/3 cup rice flour
- 1/2 teaspoon baking powder
- 1 cup rice milk
- 1/2 teaspoon vanilla essence
- 4 tablespoons caster sugar

Directions:
1. Place your air fryer on a flat kitchen surface; plug it and turn it on. Set temperature to 380 degrees F and let it preheat for 4-5 minutes.
2. Take out the air-frying basket and gently coat it using a cooking oil or spray.

3. In a bowl of medium size, thoroughly mix the ingredients except for the pineapple. Coat the pineapple slices with the batter mix.
4. Add the slices to the basket. Push the air-frying basket in the air fryer. Cook for 8 minutes.
5. Slide out the basket; top with the maple syrup, garnish with a dollop of vanilla ice cream.

Nutrition: Calories: 178 Fat: 1.7 g Carbohydrates: 38.4 g Fiber: 1.4 g Protein: 2.6 g

89. Plum Apple Crumble

Preparation time: 10-15 minutes
Cooking time: 20 minutes
Servings: 6-7
Ingredients:
- 2 ½ ounces caster sugar
- 1/3 cup oats
- 2/3 cup flour
- 1/2 stick butter, chilled
- 1 tablespoon cold water
- 1 tablespoon honey
- 1/2 teaspoon ground mace
- 1/4-pound plums, pitted and chopped
- 1/4-pound apples, cored and chopped
- 1 tablespoon lemon juice
- 1/2 teaspoon vanilla paste
- 1 cup cranberries

Directions:
1. Place your air fryer on a flat kitchen surface; plug it and turn it on. Set temperature to 390 degrees F and let it preheat for 4-5 minutes.
2. Take out the cake pan and gently coat it using a cooking oil or spray.
3. In a bowl of medium size, thoroughly mix the plums, apples, lemon juice, sugar, honey, and mace. Add the fruit mixture to the bottom of a cake pan.
4. In a bowl of medium size, thoroughly mix the remaining ingredients and top with the fruit mix.
5. Push the air-frying basket in the air fryer. Cook for 20 minutes.

6. Slide out the basket; serve warm!

Nutrition: Calories: 188 Fat: 8 g Carbohydrates: 27.8 g Fiber: 6.3 g Protein: 1.6 g

90. Creamy Banana Puffs

Preparation time: 10-15 minutes

Cooking time: 10 minutes

Servings: 8

Ingredients:
- 4 ounces instant vanilla pudding
- 4 ounces cream cheese, softened
- 1 package (8-ounce) crescent dinner rolls, refrigerated
- 1 cup milk
- 2 bananas, sliced
- 1 egg, lightly beaten

Directions:
1. Place your air fryer on a flat kitchen surface; plug it and turn it on. Set temperature to 355 degrees F and let it preheat for 4-5 minutes.
2. Unroll crescent dinner rolls and make 8 squares.
3. In a bowl of medium size, thoroughly mix the pudding and milk; whisk in the cream cheese.
4. Add the mixture in the pastry squares. Top with the slices of banana. Fold them over the filling, pressing the edges to seal. Brush each pastry puff with the whisked egg.
5. Add them to the basket. Push the air-frying basket in the air fryer. Cook for 10 minutes.
6. Slide out the basket; serve warm!

Nutrition: Calories: 307 Fat: 17 g Carbohydrates: 34.2 g Fiber: 4 g Protein: 5.6g

91. Choco-Berry Cake

Preparation Time: 10 minutes

Cooking Time: 3 minutes

Servings: 5-6

Ingredients:

- 2 eggs
- 2/3 cup all-purpose flour
- 5 tablespoons sugar
- 2/3 cup unsalted butter
- Salt as needed
- 1 cup chocolate chips, melted
- 1/3 cup raspberries

Directions:

1. Place your air fryer on a flat kitchen surface; plug it and turn it on. Set temperature to 355 degrees F and let it preheat for 4-5 minutes.
2. Take 6 ramekins and gently grease them; dust with some sugar.
3. In a bowl of medium size, thoroughly whisk the sugar and butter. Add the eggs and beat till fluffy.
4. Add the flour and salt; combine well. Add the melted chocolate chips and combine well.
5. Pour the mixture into prepared ramekins about ¾ full.
6. Add the ramekins in the basket. Push the air-frying basket in the air fryer. Cook for 3 minutes.
7. Slide out the basket; top with the raspberries and serve warm!

Nutrition: Calories: 439 Fat: 28 g Carbohydrates: 38 g Fiber: 4 g Protein: 6 g

92. Pumpkin Pie Minis

Preparation time: 25 minutes

Cooking time: 20 minutes

Servings: 12

Ingredients:

- Nutmeg (1/4 teaspoon)
- Brown sugar (3/8 cup)
- Pumpkin puree (1 cup)
- Cinnamon (1/2 teaspoon)
- Heavy cream (1 tablespoon)
- Egg, large (1 piece)
- Pie crust, refrigerated (1 package)

Directions:

1. Preheat air fryer to 325 degrees Fahrenheit.
2. Combine pumpkin, heavy cream, spices, and brown sugar.
3. Unroll dough pieces and cut out twenty-four 2.5-inch circles. Place 12 circles on sheet of parchment. Top each with pie filling (1 tablespoon) and cover with another circle. Press to seal and brush all mini pies with whisked egg (1 piece). Dust all over with mixture of cinnamon and sugar.
4. Air-fry for twenty minutes.

Nutrition: Calories 180 Fat 9.0 g Protein 1.0 g Carbohydrates 25.0 g

93. Mouthwatering Walnut Apple Pie Bites

Preparation time: 10 minutes

Cooking time: 15 minutes

Servings: 8

Ingredients:

- Brown sugar (4 tablespoons)
- Butter, melted (1 tablespoon)
- Apple, tart juicy, red, washed, sliced into 8 portions, skin on (1 piece)
- Cinnamon (3 teaspoons)

- Crescent rolls, refrigerated (1 can)
- Walnuts, chopped finely (1 ounce)

Directions:

1. Preheat air fryer to 325 degrees Fahrenheit.
2. Roll out crescent rolls onto baking sheet misted with cooking spray.
3. Brush melted butter on rolls before sprinkling with cinnamon and brown sugar. Add 3/4 of finely chopped walnuts on top; press gently to adhere. Top each of wide ends with a slice of apple, and then roll up. Brush melted butter on top of rolls before sprinkling with cinnamon and remaining 1/4 of finely chopped walnuts.
4. Air-fry for fifteen minutes.

Nutrition: Calories 49.7 Fat 3.75 g Protein 0.6 g Carbohydrates 7.6 g

94. Gooey Apple Pie Cookies

Preparation time: 15 minutes
Cooking time: 20 minutes
Servings: 12
Ingredients:

- Egg, slightly beaten (1 piece)
- Caramel sauce (1 jar)
- Flour, all purpose (2 tablespoons)
- Pie crusts, refrigerated (1 package)
- Apple pie filling (1 can)
- Cinnamon sugar (3 tablespoons)

Directions:

1. Preheat air fryer to 325 degrees Fahrenheit.
2. Roll out dough and spread thinly with caramel sauce. Chop up apple pie filling and spread over caramel sauce. Cover with strips from other rolled out dough, laid to form a lattice pattern. Cut out 3-inch cookies and arrange on baking sheet.
3. Air-fry for twenty to twenty-five minutes.

Nutrition: Calories 211.8 Fat 4.5 g Protein 1.1 g Carbohydrates 44.2 g

95. Apple Pie with Cinnamon Roll Crust

Preparation time: 15 minutes

Cooking time: 55 minutes

Servings: 16

Ingredients:

Crust:
- Butter, unsalted, melted (1 tablespoon)
- Egg, beaten (1 piece) + water (1 teaspoon)—to make egg wash
- Pie crust, refrigerated (1 package)
- Cinnamon, ground (2 teaspoons)

Pie:
- Butter, unsalted, at room temp. (1 stick)
- Apples, Granny Smith, small, peeled, cored, sliced thinly (7 pieces)
- Sugar, light brown (1 cup)
- Flour, all purpose, unbleached (1 cup)
- Granulated sugar

Icing:
- Vanilla (1/4 teaspoon)
- Milk (2 teaspoons)
- Powdered sugar (1/2 cup)
- Cinnamon, ground (1/4 teaspoon)

Directions:
1. Preheat air fryer to 375 degrees Fahrenheit.
2. Unroll pie crust; brush top with butter before sprinkling with cinnamon. Roll up and slice into half-inch rounds.
3. Press mini rolls into pie plate and brush tops with egg wash. Top with sliced apples. Cover with crumbly mixture of flour, brown sugar, and butter. Sprinkle with granulated sugar.
4. Air-fry for forty to forty-five minutes.
5. Finish by icing with whisked mixture milk, powdered sugar, cinnamon, and vanilla.

Nutrition: Calories 255 Fat 10.0 g Protein 1.5 g Carbohydrates 39.0 g

96. Sugar Cookie Cake

Preparation time: 5 minutes

Cooking time: 35 minutes

Servings: 16

Ingredients:

- Condensed milk, sweetened (14 ounces)
- Cinnamon, ground (1 teaspoon)
- Butter, salted, melted (3/4 cup)
- Cookie butter (14 ounces)
- Eggs (3 pieces)
- Sugar cookie mix, prepared (17 1/2 ounces)

Directions:

1. Preheat air fryer to 325 degrees Fahrenheit. Mist cooking spray onto baking dish.
2. Combine cookie butter with eggs, cinnamon, and condensed milk. Spread on baking dish and top with even layer of fry cookie mix. Drizzle melted butter on top and air-fry for thirty-five minutes.
3. Let cool before slicing and serving.

Nutrition: Calories 295 Fat 15.5 g Protein 4.0 g Carbohydrates 35.0 g

97. Apple Hand Pies

Preparation time: 5 minutes

Cooking time: 8 minutes

Servings: 6

Ingredients:

- 15-ounces no-sugar-added apple pie filling
- 1store-bought crust

Directions:

1. Lay out pie crust and slice into equal-sized squares.
2. Place 2 tbsp. filling into each square and seal crust with a fork.
3. Pour into the Oven rack/basket. Place the Rack on the middle-shelf of the Air fryer oven. Set temperature to 390F, and set time to 8 minutes until golden in color.

Nutrition: Calories 278 Protein 5 g Fat: 10 g. Carbs: 17 g

98. Sweet Cream Cheese Wontons

Preparation time: 5 minutes
Cooking time: 5 minutes
Servings: 16
Ingredients:
- 1 egg with a little water
- Wonton wrappers
- 1/2 C. powdered Erythritol
- 8 ounces softened cream cheese
- Olive oil

Directions:
1. Mix sweetener and cream cheese together.
2. Lay out 4 wontons at a time and cover with a dish towel to prevent drying out.
3. Place 1/2 of a teaspoon of cream cheese mixture into each wrapper.
4. Dip finger into egg/water mixture and fold diagonally to form a triangle. Seal edges well.
5. Repeat with remaining ingredients.
6. Place filled wontons into the air fryer oven and cook 5 minutes at 400 degrees, shaking halfway through cooking.

Nutrition: Calories: 303 Protein: 0.5 g Fat: 3 g Carbs: 3 g

99. Cinnamon Sugar Roasted Chickpeas

Preparation time: 5 minutes
Cooking time: 10 minutes
Servings: 2
Ingredients:
- 1 tbsp. sweetener
- 1 tbsp. cinnamon
- 1 cup chickpeas

Directions:
1. Preheat air fryer oven to 390 degrees.
2. Rinse and drain chickpeas.
3. Mix all ingredients together and add to air fryer.
4. Pour into the Oven rack/basket. Place the Rack on the middle-shelf of the Air fryer oven. Set temperature to 390F, and set time to 10 minutes.

Nutrition: Calories: 111 Protein: 16 g Fat: 19 g Carbs: 18 g

100. Brownie Muffins

Preparation time: 10 minutes
Cooking time: 10 minutes
Servings: 12
Ingredients:
- 1package Betty Crocker fudge brownie mix
- 1/4 cup walnuts, chopped
- 1 egg
- 1/3 cup vegetable oil
- 2 teaspoons water

Directions:
1. Grease 12 muffin molds. Set aside.
2. In a bowl, put all ingredients together.
3. Place the mixture into the prepared muffin molds.
4. Press "Power Button" of Air Fry Oven and turn the dial to select the "Air Fry" mode.
5. Press the Time button and again turn the dial to set the cooking time to 10 minutes.
6. Now push the Temp button and rotate the dial to set the temperature at 300 degrees F.
7. Press "Start/Pause" button to start.
8. When the unit beeps to show that it is preheated, open the lid.
9. Arrange the muffin molds in "Air Fry Basket" and insert in the oven.
10. Place the muffin molds onto a wire rack to cool for about 10 minutes.
11. Carefully, invert the muffins onto the wire rack to completely cool before serving.

Nutrition: Calories: 168 Protein: 2 g Fat: 8.9 g Carbs: 20.8 g

101. Chocolate Mug Cake

Preparation time: 15 minutes

Cooking time: 13 minutes

Servings: 1

Ingredients:
- 1/4 cup self-rising flour
- 5 tablespoons caster sugar
- 1 tablespoon cocoa powder
- 3 tablespoons coconut oil
- 3 tablespoons whole milk

Directions:
1. In a shallow mug, add all the ingredients and mix until well combined.
2. Press "Power Button" of Air Fry Oven and turn the dial to select the "Air Fry" mode.
3. Press the Time button and again turn the dial to set the cooking time to 13 minutes.
4. Now push the Temp button and rotate the dial to set the temperature at 392 degrees F.
5. Press "Start/Pause" button to start.
6. When the unit beeps to show that it is preheated, open the lid.
7. Arrange the mug in "Air Fry Basket" and insert in the oven.
8. Place the mug onto a wire rack to cool slightly before serving.

Nutrition: Calories: 729 Protein: 5.7 g Fat: 43.3 g Carbs: 88.8 g

102. Grilled Peaches

Preparation time: 10 minutes

Cooking time: 10 minutes

Servings: 2

Ingredients:
- 2 peaches, cut into wedges and remove pits
- 1/4 cup butter, diced into pieces
- 1/4 cup brown sugar
- 1/4 cup graham cracker crumbs

Directions:
1. Arrange peach wedges on air fryer oven rack and air fry at 350 F for 5 minutes.
2. In a bowl, put the butter, graham cracker crumbs, and brown sugar together.
3. Turn peaches skin side down.
4. Spoon butter mixture over top of peaches and air fry for 5 minutes more.
5. Top with whipped cream and serve.

Nutrition: Calories: 378 Protein: 2.3 g Fat: 24.4 g Carbs: 40.5 g

103. Simple and Delicious Spiced Apples

Preparation time: 10 minutes

Cooking time: 10 minutes

Servings: 4

Ingredients:
- 4 apples, sliced
- 1 tsp apple pie spice
- 2 tbsp. sugar
- 2 tbsp. ghee, melted

Directions:
1. Add apple slices into the mixing bowl.
2. Add remaining ingredients on top of apple slices and toss until well coated.
3. Transfer apple slices on instant vortex air fryer oven pan and air fry at 350 F for 10 minutes.
4. Top with ice cream and serve.

Nutrition: Calories: 196 Protein: 0.6 g Fat: 6.8 g Carbs: 37.1 g

104. Tangy Mango Slices

Preparation time: 10 minutes

Cooking time: 12 hours

Servings: 6

Ingredients:
- 4 mangoes, peel and cut into 1/4-inch slices

- 1/4 cup fresh lemon juice
- 1 tbsp. honey

Directions:

1. In a big bowl, combine together honey and lemon juice and set aside.
2. Add mango slices in lemon-honey mixture and coat well.
3. Arrange mango slices on instant vortex air fryer rack and dehydrate at 135 F for 12 hours.

Nutrition: Calories: 147 Protein: 1.9 g Fat: 0.9 g Carbs: 36.7 g

105. Peanut Butter Cookies

Preparation time: 10 minutes

Cooking time: 5 minutes

Servings: 24

Ingredients:

- 1 egg, lightly beaten
- 1 cup of sugar
- 1 cup creamy peanut butter

Directions:

1. In a big bowl, combine sugar, egg, and peanut butter together until well mixed.
2. Spray air fryer oven tray with cooking spray.
3. Using ice cream scooper scoop out cookie onto the tray and flattened them using a fork.
4. Bake cookie at 350 F for 5 minutes.
5. Cook remaining cookie batches using the same temperature.
6. Serve and enjoy.

Nutrition: Calories: 97 Protein: 2.9 g Fat: 5.6 g Carbs: 10.5 g

106. Espresso Cinnamon Cookies

Preparation time: 5 minutes

Cooking time: 15 minutes

Servings: 12

Ingredients:
- 8 tablespoons ghee, melted
- 1 cup almond flour
- 1/4 cup brewed espresso
- 1/4 cup swerve
- 1/2 tablespoon cinnamon powder
- 2 teaspoons baking powder
- 2 eggs, whisked

Directions:
1. In a bowl, mix all the ingredients and whisk well. Spread medium balls on a cookie sheet lined parchment paper, flatten them, put the cookie sheet in your air fryer and cook at 350 degrees F for 15 minutes.
2. Serve the cookies cold.

Nutrition: Calories 134 Fat 12 g Fiber 2 g Carbs 4 g Protein 2 g

107. Turmeric Almond Pie

Preparation time: 20 minutes

Cooking time: 35 minutes

Servings: 4

Ingredients:
- 4 eggs, beaten
- 1 tablespoon poppy seeds
- 1 teaspoon ground turmeric
- 1 teaspoon vanilla extract
- 1 teaspoon baking powder
- 1 teaspoon lemon juice

- 1 cup almond flour
- 2 tablespoons heavy cream
- 1/4 cup Erythritol
- 1 teaspoon avocado oil

Directions:
1. Put the eggs in the bowl. Add vanilla extract, baking powder, lemon juice, almond flour, heavy cream, and Erythritol. Then add avocado oil and poppy seeds. Add turmeric. With the help of the immersion blender, blend the pie batter until it is smooth. Line the air fryer cake mold with baking paper. Pour the pie batter in the cake mold. Flatten the pie surface with the help of the spatula if needed. Then preheat the air fryer to 365F.
2. Put the cake mold in the air fryer and cook the pie for 35 minutes. When the pie is cooked, cool it completely and remove it from the cake mold. Cut the cooked pie into the servings.

Nutrition: Calories 149 Fat 11.9 g Fiber 1.2 g Carbs 3.8 g Protein 7.7 g

108. Sponge Cake

Preparation time: 5 minutes
Cooking time: 30 minutes
Servings: 8
Ingredients:
- 1 cup ricotta, soft
- 1/3 swerve
- 3 eggs, whisked
- 1 cup almond flour
- 7 tablespoons ghee, melted
- 1 teaspoon baking powder
- Cooking spray

Directions:
1. In a bowl, combine all the ingredients except the cooking spray and stir them very well. Grease a cake pan that fits the air fryer with the cooking spray and pour the cake mix inside. Put the pan in the fryer and cook at 350 degrees F for 30 minutes.
2. Cool the cake down, slice and serve.

Nutrition: Calories 210 Fat 12 g Fiber 3 g Carbs 6 g Protein 9 g

109. Strawberry Cups

Preparation time: 5 minutes

Cooking time: 10 minutes

Servings: 8

Ingredients:
- 16 strawberries, halved
- 2 tablespoons coconut oil
- 2 cups chocolate chips, melted

Directions:
1. In a pan that fits your air fryer, mix the strawberries with the oil and the melted chocolate chips, toss gently, put the pan in the air fryer and cook at 340 degrees F for 10 minutes. Divide into cups and serve cold.

Nutrition: Calories 162 Fat 5 g Fiber 3 g Carbs 5 g Protein 6 g

110. Pecan Brownies

Preparation time: 10 minutes

Cooking time: 20 minutes

Servings: 6

Ingredients:

- 1/2 cup blanched finely ground almond flour
- 1/2 cup powdered Erythritol
- 2 tablespoons unsweetened cocoa powder
- 1/2 teaspoon baking powder
- 1/4 cup unsalted butter, softened
- 1 large egg
- 1/4 cup chopped pecans
- 1/4 cup low-carb, sugar-free chocolate chips

Directions:
1. In a large bowl, mix almond flour, Erythritol, cocoa powder, and baking powder. Stir in butter and egg.
2. Fold in pecans and chocolate chips. Scoop mixture into 6" round baking pan. Place pan into the air fryer basket.
3. Adjust the temperature to 300°F and set the timer for 20 minutes.
4. When fully cooked a toothpick inserted in center will come out clean. Allow 20 minutes to fully cool and firm up.

Nutrition: Calories: 215 Protein: 4.2 g Fiber: 2.8 g Fat: 18.9 g Sodium: 53 mg Carbohydrates: 21.8 g

111. Chocolate Banana Packets

Preparation time: 5 minutes
Cooking time: 15 minutes
Servings: 1
Ingredients:
- Miniature marshmallows (2 tablespoons)
- Cereal, cinnamon, crunchy, slightly crushed (2 tablespoons)
- Banana, peeled (1 piece)
- Chocolate chips, semi-sweet (2 tablespoons)

Directions:
1. Preheat air fryer to 390 degrees Fahrenheit.
2. Slightly open banana by cutting lengthwise. Place on sheet of foil.
3. Fill sliced banana with chocolate chips and marshmallows. Close foil packet.

4. Air-fry for fifteen to twenty minutes.
5. Open packet and top banana with crushed cereal.

Nutrition: Calories 270 Fat 7.0 g Protein 2.0 g Carbohydrates 50.0 g

112. Creamy Strawberry Mini Wraps

Preparation time: 10 minutes
Cooking time: 15 minutes
Servings: 12
Ingredients:
- Cream cheese, softened (4 ounces)
- Strawberry jam (12 teaspoons)
- Pie crust, refrigerated (1 box)
- Powdered sugar (1/3 cup)

Directions:
1. Preheat air fryer to 350 degrees Fahrenheit.
2. Roll out pie crusts and cut out 12 squares.
3. Beat together powdered sugar and cream cheese.
4. Shape each dough square into a diamond before filling with cream cheese mixture (1 tablespoon). Top each with strawberry jam (1 teaspoon) and cover with dough sides.
5. Place mini wraps on baking sheet and air-fry for fifteen minutes.

Nutrition: Calories 190 Fat 4.5 g Protein 1.0 g Carbohydrates 22.0 g

113. Heavenly Butter Cake Bars

Preparation time: 15 minutes
Cooking time: 35 minutes
Servings: 12
Ingredients:
- Butter, melted (1/2 cup)
- Cream cheese (8 ounces)
- Vanilla (1 teaspoon)

- Cake mix, super moist, French vanilla (15 1/4 ounces)
- Eggs (3 pieces)
- Powdered sugar (1 pound)

Directions:
1. Preheat air fryer to 325 degrees Fahrenheit.
2. Use parchment to line baking dish.
3. Combine cake mix with egg and melted butter to form soft dough. Press into baking dish.
4. Beat together 2 eggs, cream cheese, vanilla, and sugar. Spread on top of cake mix layer.
5. Air-fry for forty-five minutes. Let cool before slicing.

Nutrition: Calories 298.4 Fat 15.3 g Protein 2.8 g Carbohydrates 38.6 g

114. Tasty Shortbread Cookies

Preparation time: 25 minutes

Cooking time: 1 hour 35 minutes

Servings: 4

Ingredients:
- Powdered sugar (3/4 cup)
- Flour, all purpose (2 1/2 cups)
- Butter, softened (1 cup)
- Vanilla (1 teaspoon)

Directions:
1. Preheat air fryer to 325 degrees Fahrenheit.
2. Combine butter, vanilla and powdered sugar with flour to form a soft dough.
3. Roll out dough and cut out 4 circles. Place on cookie sheet.
4. Air-fry for fourteen to sixteen minutes.

Nutrition: Calories 70 Fat 4.0 g Protein 0 g Carbohydrates 7.0 g

115. Air-Fried Mini Pies

Preparation time: 20 minutes

Cooking time: 55 minutes

Servings: 4

Ingredients:
- Pie filling (4 cups)
- Pie crusts, refrigerated (2 packages)
- Egg, whisked (1 piece)

Directions:
1. Preheat air fryer to 325 degrees Fahrenheit.
2. Mist cooking spray onto 12 muffin cups.
3. Roll out pie crust and cut out twelve 4-inch circles. Press each onto bottom of a muffin cup. Cut remaining dough into thin strips.
4. Add pie filling (1/4 cup) to each dough cup. Cover each with dough strips laid in a lattice pattern.
5. Brush whisked egg on tops of pies and air-fry for thirty to forty minutes.

Nutrition: Calories 196.3 Fat 8.4 g Protein 0.7 g Carbohydrates 29.9 g

116. Ricotta Stuffed Apples

Preparation time: 10 minutes

Cooking time: 20 minutes

Servings: 4

Ingredients:
- ½ cup cheddar cheese
- ¼ cup raisins
- 2 apples
- ½ tsp ground cinnamon

Directions:
1. Preheat air fryer to 350F/177C. Combine cheddar cheese and raisins in a bowl and set aside. Chop apples lengthwise and discard the core and stem.
2. Sprinkle each half with cinnamon and stuff each half with 1/4 of the cheddar mixture. Bake for 7 minutes, turn, and bake for 13 minutes more until the apples are soft. Serve immediately.

Nutrition: Calories: 231 Carbs: 39 g Fat: 8 g Protein: 3 g

117. Banana-Almond Delights

Preparation Time: 10 minutes

Cooking time: 18 minutes

Servings: 4

Ingredients:

- 1 ripe banana, mashed
- 1 tbsp almond liqueur
- ½ tsp ground cinnamon
- 2 tbsp coconut sugar
- 1 cup almond flour
- ¼ tsp baking soda
- 8 raw almonds

Directions:

1. Preheat air fryer to 300F/150C. Add the banana to a bowl and stir in almond liqueur, cinnamon, and coconut sugar until well combined.
2. Toss in almond flour and baking soda until smooth. Make 8 balls out of the mixture.
3. Place the balls onto the parchment-lined frying basket, flatten each into ½-inch thick, and press 1 almond into the center.
4. Bake for 12 minutes, turn and bake for 6 more minutes. Let cool slightly before serving.

Nutrition: Calories: 368 Carbs: 91 g Fat: 0 g Protein: 1 g

CONCLUSION

We hope that this book has been helpful. We think that you have been able to learn some new skills about cooking with an air fryer and how to cook your favorite foods with it. One last thing before we conclude is to say goodbye and thank you for reading this book.

Goodbye!

INDEX

A

Air Fried Dragon Shrimp	41
Air Fried Mushroom Frittata	19
Air Fryer Vegetables	48
Air-Fried Mini Pies	78
Apple Hand Pies	69
Apple Pie with Cinnamon Roll Crust	68

B

Bacon and Kale Frittata	17
Bacon Butter Burgers	29
Bacon Pudding	37
Baked Eggs	15
Banana-Almond Delights	78
Basil-Garlic Breaded Chicken Bake	54
BBQ Chicken Recipe from Greece	47
Beef Bulgogi Burgers	34
Beef Satay	45
Blackened Lemon Salmon	32
Breaded Cod	53
Breakfast Baked Apple	24
Breakfast Egg Bites	14
Breakfast Ham Omelet	20
Brine-Soaked Turkey	51
Broccoli and Cheese Stuffed Chicken	35
Brownie Muffins	70

C

Cajun Chicken Fried Steak Strips	35
Cajun Salmon	59
Cheeseburger Egg Rolls	54
Chicken and Corn Casserole	38
Chicken and Zucchini Lunch Mix	39
Chicken Asian Artichoke Burgers	31
Chicken Cordon Bleu	57
Chicken Drumsticks	58
Chicken, Beans, Corn and Quinoa Casserole	40
Chili Lime Chicken Thighs	60
Choco-Berry Cake	66
Chocolate Banana Packets	76
Chocolate Mug Cake	71
Cinnamon Sugar Roasted Chickpeas	70
Citrus Blueberry Muffins	22
Coconut and Chicken Casserole	37
Coconut Lime Skirt Steak	42
Cream and Cheddar Omelet	17
Cream Sausage	11
Creamy Banana Puffs	65
Creamy Burger and Potato Bake	55
Creamy Strawberry Mini Wraps	76
Crispy Beef and Bean Tacos	32
Crispy Salt and Pepper Tofu	44
Crunchy Hash Browns	21
Crunchy Zucchini Hash Browns	21

E

Eggs in Bread Cups	16
Eggs With Chicken	18
Espresso Cinnamon Cookies	73

F

Fajita Chicken Hasselback Chicken	27
French Style Yogurt Treat	63
French Toast	20

G

Garlic Herb Butter Chicken Wings	44
Garlic Lemon Pepper Scallops	60
Gooey Apple Pie Cookies	67
Grilled Cheese Sandwich	14
Grilled Peaches	71

H

Heavenly Butter Cake Bars	77
Honey Sea Bass	42

J

Juicy Cheeseburgers	47

L

Lemon Chicken Breasts	52

M

Mac and Cheese Eggrolls	30
Meatballs Sandwich	36
Meaty Breakfast Omelet	22
Miso Glazed Salmon	52
Mongolian Shrimp	30
Mouthwatering Walnut Apple Pie Bites	67
Mushroom Eggs Morning	10
Mustard Cheese Toast	7
Mustard-Glazed Pork Tenderloin	61

N

Nuts and Seeds Granola	15

P

Pb and J Donuts	23
Peanut Butter Cookies	73
Pecan Brownies	75
Pineapple Cinnamon Treat	63

Pistachio-Crusted Chicken Breast	59
Plum Apple Crumble	64
Pork Meatballs	49
Pork Teriyaki	26
Pork Teriyaki Quesadillas	27
Potato Corn Frittata	8
Pumpkin Pie Minis	66

Q

Quick Cheese Omelet	12

R

Ricotta Stuffed Apples	78
Roasted Brussels Sprouts & Sweet Potatoes	13
Roasted Heirloom Tomato with Baked Feta	56
Roasted Potato Wedges	13
Roasted Turkey Legs	62
Roly-Poly Air Fried White Fish	40

S

Salmon and Asparagus	38
Sausage with Eggs	18
Sesame Seeds Coated Fish	50
Shrimp Southwestern Burritos	28
Simple and Delicious Spiced Apples	72
Southwest Chicken Burritos	33
Spicy Catfish	46
Spicy Lime Flank Steak	61
Spinach Bacon Frittata	11
Sponge Cake	74
Stevia -Cajun Chicken Thighs	57
Strawberry Cups	75
Sugar Cookie Cake	69
Sweet Cream Cheese Wontons	69

T

Tangy Mango Slices	72
Tasty Shortbread Cookies	77
Tofu Morning Treat	9

Tomato Cheese Sandwich	9
Tomato Spinach Frittata	12
Tuna Zucchini Melts	43
Turkish Chicken Kebab Tavuk Shish	28
Turmeric Almond Pie	74

W

Warming Winter Beef with Celery	48
Wondrous Creole Fried Shrimp with Sriracha Sauce	50

Y

Yummy Bagel Morning	7

Made in the USA
Las Vegas, NV
31 January 2023